Thirty Something Millionaire

CHANGE YOUR MINDSET TO MAXIMIZE YOUR WEALTH

Cory Roberts

Cory Roberts
Denver, Colorado
www.thirtysomethingmillionaire.com

Book Layout ©2017 BookDesignTemplates.com
Editor: Jill Welsh
Cover Design: Melissa Perkins

Thirty Something Millionaire/ Cory Roberts. —1st ed.

Contents

Acknowledgements

First and foremost, I would like to thank my wife, Treslyn. The front of this book has one name on it, but it should have two. We started this journey together and this entire project was completed together. While we are both very busy with our real jobs, Treslyn and I spent countless hours on weekends and weeknights working to make this brand a reality. As I'm writing this now, Treslyn is on a plane to Philadelphia for work. She is working on Thirty Something Millionaire on her flight and I'm at home wrapping up a couple more changes. If we didn't have each other while we were barricaded in our house, working on this project, eating junk food, it would have never become a reality.

I would like to thank our parents and all our family members for supporting us through this journey. It's a roller coaster of emotions when you set out on an entrepreneurial journey. One day you are excited about progress and the next day you question if what you are doing is worth it. Your encouragement and positive comments motivated us every step of the way.

To our extended family and friends. Thank you for staying with us through the countless times we had to cancel plans to work on the book. Also, a special thank you to everyone who took time to read drafts of the book and supply necessary edits and critiques. Some really took it upon themselves to put in a lot of time with edits, you know who you are, and I cannot tell you how much we appreciate you.

I would like to thank our editor, Jill Welsh, who worked with us since the beginning of this project. Treslyn and I are not English majors, we work in finance, and this really showed in our first, very rough, draft. Jill helped us mold the book and create structure. Organizing scattered words on a page into a book.

Last but not least, I would like to thank you for picking up this book. Your support means the world to us. If we can help inspire one person, this project was a success.

Introduction

Everyone will have a different reason for sitting down and reading material on personal finance. You may be reading because you want to start your journey to financial freedom, or maybe you are someone (like me) who is interested in learning about different tools, tactics, and opinions about personal finance. I would like to start by saying the core principles of this book will be consistent with most of the "best practices" out there. But, the "best practices" are missing a key component to financial freedom: *How to be financially fit while still living a full life*. There are millions of different opinions, articles, and self-help books about how to structure your finances. Most of the information just talks numbers: save X% of your income and invest in low-cost mutual funds, market indexes, target funds, etc. We all know the formula for financial freedom, but the key point missing today is: *How do I accomplish my financial goals without putting my life on hold?*

Going down the road to financial freedom does not mean you have to put your current life on hold. Being financially free does not involve eliminating all the things you love in life to just sit on the floor in your living room with the heat off, the lights off and staring at the wall doing nothing all in the spirit of saving money. That's extreme, but I think you get the picture. Coming from someone who is obsessed with life and living it to the fullest, as well as being obsessed with financial freedom, you don't have to limit your life to become financially free. And, you don't have to limit your life because of money, you just need to change how you think about money. I want to fill you in on the techniques to live the life of your dreams while accelerating down the road to financial freedom.

Let's get some facts straight as we dive in. My wife and I are not trust fund babies. We have not had money given to us, and we don't work in exclusive upper-tier jobs. The real differentiator for us, and how we are able to break away from the pack, is living a *financially fit* life. In our lives we do everything we have always dreamed of and can still save more than most people even dream about. They say you can't have your cake and eat it too? I would beg to differ!

During this journey, I have learned that money doesn't buy happiness. Sure, it can buy things that will make you happy for a bit, but it will not make you a happy person or give you any type of sustained happiness. If you're a miserable person with little money, you will still be miserable with more money. Living what we like to call a financially fit life will make you happier, reduce stress, and help you build wealth. The primary focus of this book is to help you learn about yourself, your passions and how to save money. This will allow you to align your spending in a way that maximizes both. This alignment, coupled with a small tweak to your habits and understanding the correct way to think about money will transform your financial world. You will spend less but feel like you are getting more... Now that is a deal.

So what is my proposition to the world? I want to make a real difference in people's lives. This book is *not* the "Top five things that wealthy people don't want you to know," or "The bulletproof guide to becoming a millionaire in a year." Any get-rich-quick scheme is simply that: a scheme.

What Is Financial Fitness?

Financial fitness (noun): spending money only on things that add value to your life, and saving the rest.

A financially fit person will only spend money on things that add value to their lives, say "no" to everything else, and invest the rest. These types of people will strive for consistency in their lives and make it a priority never to change their lifestyle because of money. What you see as valuable will change throughout life, but so will the things you don't value. The goal is to consistently revisit this conversation with yourself, and align your spending and saving in that direction.

Price Is What You Pay; Value Is What You Get

Financial fitness is a complete transformation; you have to live and breathe it. This is not a crash-course plan that you stay on for a week, and by the end of the week you say, "Forget it." It means pausing to decide whether something you think you want will add value to your life before you spend your hard-earned money. As you read the real-life examples later in the book, focus on yourself and think about how to adapt those practices in your life.

How do you achieve this without giving up everything? Financially fit people never say "no" due to a lack of money. These people get creative in how they approach things and experiences that enrich their lives. With a magnifying glass on what actually matters every second, and the knowledge of how to build wealth, a financially fit person goes to extremes to do what they love *and* hit their financial targets. You will be shocked at how far your money can actually go when you adopt this change in mindset.

What do you want in life? I'll bet you would rather travel around the world instead of working. How do you make that desire a reality? How do you set yourself up for this? None of this happens overnight. No self-help book will make that a reality in a year...sorry to burst your bubble.

The real problem is that people have a tendency to overestimate the future without focusing on the short term. Long-term wealth is obtained by making small progress each day. The short-term progress will often go unnoticed, but the compounding effect of all the small progress is what will make you wealthy. Rome was not built in a day, but if you stack one stone on top of another every day, you will end up building a city.

While long-term goals are important, focusing on your process to achieve short-term goals is more important. Your goal could be to have $1 million dollars, but it's your daily process or habits that will ultimately get you to that goal. My objective is to empower you on your personal finance journey, and to guide you through the correct process for building wealth. Next, I will share my personal journey to financial fitness. If you want to dive into the nuts and bolts of structuring your personal finances, skip to the next section (but you will miss some rather funny and embarrassing stories).

My Road to Financial Fitness

It is said that it takes 10,000 hours to become an expert at anything. 10,000 hours is a lot of time. If you do something for 12 hours a day, it would take around 2.5 years to hit 10,000 hours. Now 12 hours a day, every day, for almost 2.5 years is not realistic. But let's say you did something for an hour a day. How long would it take to become an expert? If my math is correct, it would take you over twenty-seven years. Since a young age, I have been passionate about personal finance and being financially fit. Have I put in my 10,000 hours to become an expert on financial fitness? Yes. In fact, I hit the 10,000 hour mark early in my adult life.

In conversations with friends and family, I always end up talking about money. People want to understand how I can do the things I do while remaining on a strict budget. At the end of the conversation, I always hear the same two comments: "I'm going to create a budget and stick to it," and "You should write a book about this." As someone who downplays any success in my life, calling myself an "expert" feels odd, because I'm not an expert investor, money manager, or finance guru. I'm just a normal guy who is an expert at doing a lot with a little. I've had this mindset ever since I can remember. When I could stand on my own, I started putting in my 10,000 hours: day in and day out. I learned how to get what I wanted in life by spending the least amount of money so I could keep growing my savings.

I never say "no" to anything I love; my current passions are traveling the world, buying cars, snowboarding, mountain biking… the list goes on and on. I do all these things on the same budget I built for myself out of college. Yes, my income is higher than my first job out of college, but I love the life I live, so why change anything? I never want money to dictate my decisions, because I never want money to control me. What do I seek in life? Value. I like value. Actually, I love value. Whether it's on experiences or new shoes. After putting in my 10,000 hours to become more knowledgeable, my mind is incapable of thinking any other way. Because of this, I only chase what I love, and in chasing what I love, I end up doing what I love because I don't let anything else enter my mind unless it brings "value" to my life. I'm never distracted by items that take value out of my life. My money speaks the same language. Due to this habit, I receive sustained happiness because I have eliminated whatever is out of alignment with my happiness. Money is an important resource, and once you take control of it, you can take control of your life.

Ever since I could remember, I have saved money. I believe the origin of this comes from how I was raised. My parents worked in the corporate world in sales-related jobs and were successful. They had the money to spoil their children and give us all kinds of things, but they didn't. They only spent money on things that brought value to my life (sports, school activities, travel, etc.). If I wanted a pair of jeans, they would buy me what I needed; which was not what I wanted (think Walmart not Nordstrom's). If I wanted a pair of jeans that were more expensive or a "luxury" in their eyes, I had to save up and buy them myself. My parents gave me all the opportunities in the world, but I knew if I wanted extras I had to work for them, and that stuck with me.

I began working at a golf course when I was thirteen. My parents' first rule, instilled from my grandma, Zakea, was to save half of each paycheck. I could spend the rest. I cannot remember what I made, probably around $6.00 per hour. What really changed my perspective about money, though, was looking at how small my paycheck was after working for two weeks. I didn't want to spend a dime because I'd worked in the hot sun every day to earn it. I equated each dollar I spent to the time and effort put forth to earn it. My parents never had to save half of my paycheck for me; I took this task upon myself and saved it all.

I was a little obsessed, okay a lot obsessed—maybe it was the rap music I listened to—but I would cash my paycheck and put the money under my bed wrapped in a rubber band. I'm not 100% sure why I didn't use a bank account. Don't put your money under your mattress; it's not FDIC insured under there! From time to time I would take it out of the rubber band to count it. Sometimes I would lock my door and throw it in the air. After throwing it in the air, I would immediately count it again to make sure it was all accounted for and then restore it to "safety" under my mattress.

What did I do with the money I saved when I was younger? Well I was really into snowboarding and loved going to a snowboard camp in Oregon every summer. The deal my parents made with me was that they would buy my flight from Colorado to Oregon as my birthday gift, and I covered the cost of the camp. I looked forward to that camp all year. I relived the memories from that trip until the following year when I would go back again. If I didn't save my money, I didn't get to go. This core principle my parents taught me was so valuable. As a kid you want your parents to buy you everything you see; however, that accomplishes nothing but enabling your child. They will never to be able to stand up financially without some sort of a crutch. This parenting strategy taught me to make value purchases with my money early on, which has become the baseline for everything in my life.

I'm very thankful for the way I was raised because now I only focus on what makes me happy, and that is where my money goes. Giving money to your kids for everything teaches them absolutely nothing. Open the door for them, give them everything they need (not want), and watch them succeed. By making these selected gestures they will have all the opportunities and the skill set to embark on the journey to obtaining what they want.

As a side note, my parents are now retired with more than enough money to live comfortably. Are they changing how they live now? Do they buy lots of luxury items and go out to all the top restaurants? The answer is no. They are still laser-focused on what makes them happy and spend their money accordingly, it's engrained in their DNA. I don't believe there is any correlation to how much you should spend based on how much you have. My dad loves to shop at consignment stores and appreciates a good deal. It's now a competition between us on who can get the greatest value out of a dollar. We swap stories about how we got a deal here or how we got an item for free. Maybe if you saw him in a consignment store trying to save an extra dollar on something, you might think he's hurting for cash, but he isn't. Perception is not reality. My dad will walk out of the consignment store with his new $12 shirt that retails for $75. Next he'll step onto his forty-foot sailboat, which he paid for in cash, docked in a San Diego yacht club. My parents love to sail but don't care about fashion. Now *that* is value purchasing.

I would not call myself cheap, but if you ask any of my friends, ten times out of ten they will say I'm cheap. I prefer the word frugal. I just spend money on things I see value in like hobbies, travel, etc. Most don't quite understand that value proposition. Maybe they don't see value in the same things I do, or maybe they just spend money without thinking about the value impact to their lives (I bet it is mostly the latter, and a little of the former). The things people see value in are like a fingerprint: it's different for everyone.

I have worked since I was thirteen. In high school, I worked every day after school and had two jobs in the summer. I learned early that money is not easy to make, and it's even harder to keep. I went to extremes to save, which really dialed in my skills to be financially fit. I'm going to embarrass myself a bit and talk about a young, up-and-coming financially fit man... here come some fun stories. After each story, I'll summarize why I did those things and why it relates to the core of this book: spend money on the things and experiences that enrich your life or in which you perceive value.

Don't get the wrong idea, I would never recommend the following practices to anyone. They are simply funny and rather humiliating things I did as a youth to save or make money. Maybe you can use some of the ideas in your own life.

Making Money on Golf Balls

I have been playing golf since I was six years old. Guess how much I have spent on golf balls? If you guessed $0, you would be correct—and it's not because I'm good at golf. Every time I lost a ball, I would head into the area where the ball disappeared and find several more. The golf course I worked at had a lot of scrub oak and dense forest off the fairway, so people lost a lot of golf balls. Most never cared to go in a look for them. The out-of-bounds areas were loaded with golf balls, especially after tournaments. Most Mondays, the course would put on a big tournament, usually as an outing for a large company or a fundraiser. Just because it's a tournament didn't mean the people had skills on the course. Newsflash: most players buy expensive golf balls at the pro shop and proceed to lose them somewhere between the first tee and the eighteenth hole. This is as true today as it was back then.

After each tournament, my dad and I would grab a backpack after everyone left the course and comb through the forest for golf balls. We knew the right places to look and we would walk our route searching for golf balls. This accomplished three things:

1. Our golf ball supply at home was large, ensuring we never paid for a golf ball.
2. It allowed me to start my first business selling golf balls.
3. I got to spend quality time with my dad.

I would store a supply of balls to sell in between the twelfth and thirteenth holes on the course. During busy weekends, and especially on those tournament days, I would sell the slightly used balls to the golfers. They always wanted to support me as a young entrepreneur, and many times they would have lost so many that they needed more to finish their round. After I wrapped up selling for the day, my dad and I would head out that night and find all the golf balls they lost again.

On tournament Mondays in the summer, I would get to the course early for work, helping to set up the carts and the driving range. Once that was complete, I greeted people in the parking lots and took their bags to the cart (making tips!). During the tournament I sold the aforementioned used golf balls, and afterward I would clean people's clubs (for tips) and also take bags back to the car (again, for tips).

Moral of this story: don't ever pay for a golf ball. Golf can be expensive, but this is one way to really cut down the cost. I'm not telling you that you need to sit on the course every weekend to sell golf balls, but rather each time you lose a ball, head into the woods and find two. Why pay for them when you can find them for free? The activity of playing golf is what you love, not a fancy golf ball in my opinion. When you find golf balls in the woods, throw away all the crappy ones (you don't need that kind of negativity in your life). I personally like to play with only Titleist Pro-V1s from the forest. It all comes down to adding value to your life without spending money. For the rest of my life, on principal, I will never ever pay for a golf ball, and I plan to play golf as long as I am able.

Snowboarding, Free Lodging, and Free Food

When I was younger, I wanted to snowboard every weekend but didn't want to spend any money. Once I turned sixteen, I had a car and could drive to the mountains to pursue my passion. I loved it, and it was all that I thought about. If you have ever skied in Colorado, you know that the roads can get really icy from bad weather, and there is a high volume of people driving to the ski resorts. Needless to say, it was a grind doing day trips to the mountains from Denver. Traffic was horrible, and it took a lot of gas to go back and forth. Not to mention wear and tear on the car: tires, brakes etc. Not only was it a pain to make the trip, it was also expensive.

My solution involved several things. First, I needed a place to stay for the night, and I was not about to pay for a hotel room. One night, my buddy's parents got us a hotel room at a place in Frisco, Colorado. That night we stayed up really late in the lobby and noticed the lobby was in an entirely different area than the front desk. It was 2:00 a.m., and we started talking. Why not just crash on the couch in that lobby? We hadn't seen a person walk by since 9:00 p.m. So one weekend we gave it a shot. We packed our bags and headed to the hills for the weekend with no place to stay. We ended up partying that night in the lobby, sneaking into the "entertainment" area of the hotel, which had a pool, hot tub, and arcade room.

We had a jug of Mountain Dew and some red Solo cups. We put our pocket change in the pool table and had enough money for one game, we paid and the billiard balls were dispensed from the table. Since we only had enough money for one game, I came up with the rather brilliant idea to just drink the Mountain Dew out of the bottle and put the red Solo cups into the pool pockets. When the ball went into the pocket we could just snag it and put it aside so we wouldn't have to pay for another round of pool. We played pool all night and only had to pay for one game. I'm sure we hit the hot tub and the sauna also. All the lights were shut off in the lobby and around 2:00 a.m. we decided to call it a night. We intentionally slept on the couches whose backs faced the front so if anyone walked by they would not see us. The next morning we woke up, brought all our ski stuff inside, and put it by the fire to warm up. There was coffee out front, which we sipped as we prepared to go snowboarding.

It was a very transformational time for me. Who needed to buy a place in the mountains or pay for a hotel room? We did this every weekend, but the story goes a little deeper than that. You could call me cheap at this age, but I really didn't have much money and wanted to live the snowboard lifestyle. Not paying for a hotel room was a great start, but I wanted to go further than that. Have you ever purchased food at a ski resort? Let me tell you, it's not affordable. So what was my solution? Please don't judge too much, because all my friends ended up doing exactly the same thing after seeing my success.

My parents bought me a season pass at the ski resort for my Christmas gift, but everything else was up to me, including lunch at the resort. After skiing all morning, I needed some fuel and loved the food at the resort; I just didn't want to pay for it. And, no, I didn't steal anything. I'm frugal, but not a criminal. One day we were all sitting around a large group of kids who had way more food than they could eat. At the same time I was making my favorite dish at the ski resort, which was tomato soup with crackers and butter. The hot water, ketchup packets, saltine crackers, and butter were all for free. So I would pour hot water into a large cup, put in tons of ketchup packets and a touch of honey, and then grab loads of crackers and butter to fuel up. Believe me, this free "tomato" soup got old fast.

While I was eating my usual, I saw some kids who were about to throw away half the food they'd purchased while getting all their gear ready to head back out to the slopes. My cheap (and hungry) light bulb illuminated in my brain. I was not about to let those kids throw away perfectly good pizza, french fries, and boneless wings. As they were packing up, and to my friend's amazement, I asked the parents if I could finish off the kids' food. They gave me a very weird look, but I could've cared less about what people thought, and they said I could take the food.

As my friends were eating the free granola bars they hand out at the resort, I was diving deep into a five-course meal. Needless to say, everyone was a bit jealous, but they were not yet at the point to imitate what I had done. This, was my new thing. That was probably one of the best lunches I ever had while snowboarding. Each weekend I would do the same thing: walk around the cafeteria like a bald eagle looking for prey (people that were ready to leave and had a bunch of food they didn't eat). I would cut off the pieces with teeth marks and bring my catch back to the table.

After a few times, my friends had had enough of watching me eat at the top of the food chain and wanted some for themselves. As we walked into the cafeteria I got a lot of questions about how I managed to get so much food. So we sat down at a table and I laid out my tactics, developing a plan for us all to eat like kings. I dispatched my friends to all sides of the cafeteria and told them to look for families that were putting on their ski outfits who still had food on the table. I had my team dispersed, waiting and watching. I told everyone to grab the big items and put them on a new plate. Once the plate had filled up, you were allowed to come back to the table. I gathered my share and headed back to our table. To my amazement, everyone brought back way more food than we could all eat. We put everything in the middle of the table and began to feast. It was like Thanksgiving Day every weekend. Sleeping for free in hotel lobbies, using all the amenities, and eating for free at the resort. What a life! I cannot even begin to account for all the money we saved by doing these things. On top of it all, we were living the life that people save up for all year to take this type of vacation. The main difference for us was that it didn't cost us a dime.

I'm married now, and I don't think "hotel surfing" would fly anymore, but my friends and I had a blast during those years. Ironically, I went from sleeping in hotel lobbies to now owning a condo near the ski resorts that I rent out on Airbnb. It pays for itself so it's still free, but in a more grown-up way.

The moral of these stories is to focus on what *you* love and figure out how you can do it without spending a bunch of money. Would you rather ski for two days a year or ski as much as you want for the same amount of money? Center your attention on whatever adds value to your trip and strip everything else away. You are still going to ski, which is what you will love and remember the most, so don't spend money on other useless things.

A Millionaire Defined

You might not think that some kid who slept in the lobby of a hotel and asked for leftover food would be millionaire material, right? Well the habit of seeking both passion and value has put me on the road to becoming a millionaire and achieving financial freedom. But let's take a step back for a minute; what is a millionaire?

The true definition of a millionaire is an individual or household that has over $1 million dollars in net worth. Net worth is the value of the assets you own minus the total dollar amount of debt that you owe. When you see someone with a brand-new, fancy car with a loan that is more than the car is worth, who drives up to a house that is 100% financed (no equity), that person might *look* like a millionaire. The truth of the matter is that they most likely have a negative net worth. Debt is a powerful drug. Debt is like steroids—its sole purpose is to create a fake external image, while your health and your finances are probably rotting away. Perception is not reality.

A great book to read after this one is *The Millionaire Next Door*.[1] In summary, the authors wanted to write a book on the spending and living habits of people who are *worth* a million dollars. The key word here is *worth*. What they found may shock you. The people living in the big houses with the fancy cars, the people you would think are millionaires were not actually worth $1 million. However, the people living in modest homes and driving modest cars had the most wealth.

Did you know, according to the National Endowment for Financial Education, around 70% of people who win the lottery end up bankrupt within five years?[2] *Sports Illustrated* once estimated that 78% of NFL players are either

---

Thomas Stanley and William Danko, *The Millionaire Next Door* (Lanham, MD: Taylor Trade Publishing, 1996).

Ryan Hart, "What Percentage of Lottery Winners Go Broke? (Plus 35 More Statistics)," December 3, 2018, **https://www.ryanhart.org/lottery-winner-statistics/**.

bankrupt or under financial stress within two years of leaving the league?[3] Why do lottery winners and professional athletes go broke at such an alarming rate? They are rich, right? However, if someone is making a large amount of money without good financial habits, they probably won't know how to manage money. Therefore, they will probably lose that money.

In order for the people you see living lavish lives to retain net worth, they would need to be making an exorbitant amount of money, and the U.S. income statistics show otherwise.[4] Like I said before, you don't become wealthy from spending. That is why I think it's so strange that people correlate high spending to wealth. Wealthy people are actually quite frugal.

Throw out your old preconceptions about what it means to be rich, because there is no consistent answer or idea for what that looks like. To me, a rich person is someone who only spends money on things that add value to their lives and only partakes in activities they love and are passionate about. These people think about every dollar they spend because they don't want to waste their money; they know that wasted money is a waste of their freedom. A person who lives like that will accumulate both cash and memories. A bank full of money and a bank full of memories from doing what you love is the definition of rich to me.

Accumulating money is certainly part of becoming a millionaire, but the act of accumulating wealth comes down to a change in behavior. You can have all the ingredients to make a fabulous meal, but if you don't follow the recipe, you might not end up with the meal you envisioned. Being financially fit requires a change in mindset, which will lead to a change in habits and behavior. These transformations will have a massive impact on your life. Self-made millionaires are people who took the long road, eliminated wasteful

---

The undefeated.com, Rodney Brooks, "Why Do So Many Pros Go Broke?" March 24, 2017, https://theundefeated.com/features/why-do-so-many-pros-go-broke/.
Wallethacks.co, Jim Wang, "Average Income in America: What salary in the United States puts you in the top 50%, top 10%, and top 1%?" June 20, 2019, https://wallethacks.com/average-median-income-in-america/.

spending to allocate toward passions, and only spent money on things that added tremendous value to their life. This allowed them to invest the rest.

You will regret not living for the now, and you will most definitely regret not saving more. Learn how to do both.

Why Do So Many People Struggle with Money?

Similar to the diet industry, there are millions of books and articles about how to get in shape and lose weight fast. The diet industry and the personal finance industry have much in common. How do you lose weight? Simply take a look at the recommended calorie intake for your age group and height, then consume a balanced diet that hits the target calorie intake each day, and exercise thirty minutes three to five days a week. Easy, right?

How do you become financially fit? Don't spend more than you make.

Cool, we are done...

Then why do so many people struggle with both of those concepts? Because many people tend to overestimate the future, and as a result, they neglect to act today.

People believe things will happen in the future without making the effort in the present. Wake up! Don't overestimate the future without a plan. If there is no plan to get to your desired future, you will never achieve your goals. How many times have you heard or thought the following?

- Just one more cigarette, then I will quit.
- Just one more slice of cake tonight and I will never have another slice again.
- My diet starts tomorrow.
- I will save 15% of my paycheck next month.

Things really get interesting when you add money into the equation. If you ask someone where they think they will be in twenty years, you will most likely get an extremely overinflated answer. If you narrow the question and ask how much money they think they will have, you will get another unrealistic answer. But if you ask them *how* they plan to accumulate that amount, they usually cannot articulate an answer.

This is why people keep throwing their money away on useless things with no real impact (value) on their lives. Just like a person on a "diet," shoving ice cream into their mouth, who says, "I'm going to look so good in a bathing suit this summer." The person who says they will be wealthy later in life keeps telling themselves: "I will contribute more to my 401(k) next month." Or, "I will start reducing my debt next year." You need to understand that every dollar, just like every calorie, counts and has an impact on tomorrow, next year, and thirty years from today.

Challenge the Status Quo

Did you know, according to Bankrate.com, the median net worth for households in the United States at retirement age is less than $192,000? The median net worth for households in the United States aged thirty-five and under is around $11,000.[5] These statistics even include the equity wrapped in a home. This is very scary. Think about this fact from CareerBuilder: "Seventy-eight percent of full-time workers are living paycheck to paycheck."[6]

Don't settle for the status quo because the status quo is broken. These statistics are absolutely shocking. It's terrifying how financially unstable many people are, which is why more folks are continuing to work later in life and might not ever be able to retire. Time is your best friend. Don't be the person behind the counter at age sixty. As you get older, panic may start to set in because the older you get, the harder it becomes to build enough wealth to sustain your lifestyle.

How do you break through and challenge the status quo to build wealth? Knowledge and habits. Which do you think is more important? I would venture that 20% is knowledge and habits are 80%. The education side of

Bankrate.com, Adrian Garcia, "This is the median Net Worth by age — how do you compare?" February 7, 2019, **https://www.bankrate.com/personal-finance/median-net-worth-by-age/**.

Morningalliance.com, Rho Lall, "Achieving Financial Freedom Is a Marathon, 2018, http://www.morningalliance.com/category/saving/.

personal finance is straight forward, and we will walk through many of the core principles in this book. I will share innovative ways to structure your financial world and how to think about money. We will also dive into some of the largest purchases in life and how to approach them. That knowledge is important because financial mistakes can be costly, but they are easily avoidable. First let's focus on the biggest contributor to wealth: habits.

People are not bad with money because they aren't smart; people are bad with money because they haven't learned how to create positive habits surrounding money. A small tweak to your habits will open the door to a better life lived while still accumulating a net worth you can thrive on later. That is a win/win!

Challenge the status quo by thinking differently about money in every situation. Are you the type of person who likes to have control over your life, both now and in the future? I think it's safe to say we all do. The first step to changing your habits is understanding why the status quo exists.

CHAPTER 1

Habits are the Foundation of Wealth

Habits are the secret sauce to success. The first step in getting to a new destination is just that...the first step. The key is to keep striving for one more step. Before you know it, you will be living in a completely different world.

Status quo (noun): the existing state of affairs (Merriam Webster)

Your habits have created your status quo. When you're young, everything takes a significant amount of time. You are exploring the world and figuring out what works and what doesn't. As you learn what works, your brain creates express pathways for those habits to free up space in your mind for more complex tasks. Most habits you don't even think about, such as putting the right leg of your pants on first, or taking the same route to work every day. Have you ever been on your way to work only to "wake up" and realize you don't remember passing through a particular part of town?

How Habits Are Formed

Habits are reinforced through repetition. You have driven to work a countless number of times which is why you no longer pay attention to the details along the way. Most of the things you do are on autopilot, and that may be the reason you have developed poor spending habits. There is a lot of psychology going on in regards to habits.

Your brain's goal is to automate and simplify tasks to free up processing power for complex tasks. If you still had to think through the process of tying your shoes each day, humans would not be building rocket ships. Clearly autopilot has its benefits. As you reinforce specific actions, hardwired pathways are created in your brain. The more you repeat these actions, the more comfortable the brain feels in automating those activities. A path emerges. Through reinforcement that path becomes a highway. The highway has a known destination, it seems safe, and the brain repeats that action. Enough repetition and you no longer think about performing those specific actions. These pathways become your current habits. Your brain doesn't necessarily know what is actually good for you, it only knows what feels safe and comfortable. Your brain follows the path of least resistance...your status quo.

Your brain will always try to re-route you if you decide to take a different approach to an ingrained habit; it automatically wants to revert to the path of least resistance. That new action will send distress signals, saying, *do not enter*—even if that change is good for you.

Think about how hard it is to quit smoking. Most people realize that smoking is terrible for your health, so why does the brain freak out when you take it away? Apart from the fact that nicotine is highly addictive, your brain doesn't want to stop smoking, even if that change is beneficial. It's a survival mechanism hardwired into our brains: we like to walk a familiar path because we know it's safe, it is comfortable.

It's not our fault; this is human nature, but you *can* break the cycle. Poor money habits are a product of reinforced actions over time. Your brain feels comfortable repeating actions such as having a car payment, pushing off savings goals, or spending freely on whatever your heart desires. Many of these actions are completed on autopilot without any conscious thought, just like that car trip to work.

Changing Bad Habits

Don't be afraid of change. Even though it may seem daunting at first, it will eventually become your new normal. Your brain likes your current routine. It wants to feel good in the moment, and because of that, your brain is resistant to change. Change is good. Someone who is addicted to unhealthy food, for example, will have a consistent flow of electrical pulses telling them they are hungry and must eat whether they are hungry or not. Each time they eat, the brain relaxes because it likes that type of food, so changing that cycle will send off distress signals. The only way to change is to put up a detour sign and head down your new chosen path...for the next hour, two hours, a day, a week, a month, and then forever. The detour behavior is now the preferred path, and suddenly, your brain recognizes that new path.

The first time down that path you will start to mat the grass down. The more you walk the new path, the more your brain likes it because it's recognizable. Keep walking that new path and a trail will start to form. The old path will start to sprout grass because it's no longer being used. Soon enough, the old path is overgrown and a new highway emerges: your new habit.

Creating positive money habits requires a conscious effort to pave that new highway. You may have poor money habits coming out of college or think money doesn't matter now because you are not making very much of it. You have grown accustomed to debt and look at the debt statistics in this country to make yourself feel better. You tell yourself you can change the behavior later. But you need to forge a new path *now*, because positive money habits are the foundation of wealth.

If you are interested in learning more about building habits and the psychology behind them, be sure to read *Atomic Habits* by James Clear.[7]

Being financially fit is not something you are born with. You are born with the instinct to survive by finding food and shelter. The ability to manage

---

[7] James Clear, *Atomic Habits* (New York: Avery, 2018).

money and grow your net worth comes from a little knowledge and a lot of habit.

Do you want to know why the rich get richer and the poor get poorer? It's because many people, regardless of their incomes, have poor money habits. If everyone's pay doubled tomorrow, they would simply spend three times as much. Yes, three times as much, even though their pay only doubled. It is not about how much you make, it is about your habits. If you want to change your financial future, you need to change your current behavior, i.e., your habits.

It purportedly takes over a month to form a new habit. When it comes to money matters, however, I disagree. Given the appropriate effort, I believe it only takes a week to change the trajectory of your behavior as it relates to your finances. This week of different behavior will start to forge a new path in your brain.

The initial change is the hardest part. Even if you don't believe this is true, try something new for a week, and during that week let that new habit consume you; make it all you think about. After a week, it will feel odd *not* doing it. The longer you repeat an activity, the more your brain will like it and dislike other actions. Once you start to perform a set of actions, your brain will want you to repeat those actions, and boom, a new and better behavior is formed.

You will be amazed at what a plan and a habit can accomplish. Don't be fooled by get-rich-quick books, workshops, or courses. Building wealth is accomplished by building the correct habit and financial plan, not necessarily a large income. While making a plan is easy; execution is what's important. Meaning that if you don't make some important changes now, you could fall into the average of the statistic quoted earlier. With a few simple tweaks to your daily habits, you can grow well beyond this statistic.

Creatures of Habit and Masters of Execution

Creating positive money habits will change you as a person. You will create the money habits of real millionaires. Do you think millionaires become wealthy by spending money frivolously? No, millionaires are creatures of habit and masters of execution. They set long-term goals, but form habits that focus 100% on small daily wins. They only spend when the price and the perception of value align. A millionaire knows that $15 dollars is not a lot of money. But a millionaire also knows that saving $15 dollars a day, every day for thirty-five years with compounded interest can turn into $1,000,000.

How? Good financial habits and compound interest. Compound interest will be discussed in greater depth in a later chapter. If you focus on having $1 million, and that is all you think about, you will never achieve that goal. That million is comprised of many tiny (often unnoticeable) wins every minute. If you adopt a habit of hitting your short-term goals, you will consistently build net worth, and small actions over time are how you get to $1 million. Focus on your habits today, and become a master of execution to achieve that larger end goal. Good financial practices and compound interest carried out together are the simple equation to financial freedom.

Make a Plan

Later in the book I will walk you through exactly how to build the only budget you will ever need. I will also teach you how to calculate and grow your net worth. Before we dive into all that, let me explain why a plan is crucial. First, a plan is not a restriction; a plan is a financial path. As long as you are on that path, you can rest easy at night because you know where you will be financially at the end of this month, the next month, and the end of the year.

Imagine how much stress you can remove from your life by developing a roadmap for your finances. Do you ever stress about having enough money at the end of the month? End of the year? In retirement? If I told you that you can completely avoid that, would you do it? You might be thinking it involves someone with an advanced or technical finance background. Let me be the first to tell you that building a budget is basic. Sticking to your budget? That is 98% of the work, and it all comes down to changing a few habits/behaviors. Being successful with money actually has nothing to do with money. You need to set a behavior and repeat it; it's that easy.

CHAPTER 2

Scary vs. Dangerous

I want to tell you about a really cool statement I heard when listening to a podcast called "How I Built This" with Guy Raz. Mr. Raz was interviewing the founder of Samuel Adams, Jim Koch, who talked about the differences between scary and dangerous things in life. These are Jim's examples from the podcast:

Scary, but not dangerous: Rappelling off a cliff. It's very scary to strap yourself to a rope and walk backward off a huge cliff. It's not dangerous though, because that rope could hold the weight of a car. Another example is the fear of flying. The thought of hurtling through the air at 500 mph at 30,000 feet inside of a tube of steel could seem scary, but it's not dangerous. Statistically, airline travel is actually one of the safest forms of transportation.

Dangerous, but not scary: Walking through fresh snow in the backcountry on a 35-degree slope at 10,000 feet in the Rocky Mountains. It's March, with a bright-blue sky overhead. It is not scary at all, but it is very dangerous. Why is this dangerous? Snow is starting to melt, and eventually, that melting snow will find a layer of ice below the surface. In case you didn't know, fresh snow atop these conditions is a recipe for an avalanche.

It's the dangerous but not scary things that have massive potential negative impacts. These are the silent killers so to speak.

Jim Koch related dangerous but not scary to his early career. When talking about why he wanted to start his own business in the podcast interview, Mr. Koch said, "Staying at BCG (Boston Consulting Group) was dangerous, but not scary. The danger, the risk of it, was continuing to do something that didn't make me happy, and getting to sixty-five and looking back and go...oh my God, I wasted my life. *That* is risk; *that* is danger."

Ask yourself these questions:

- Financially, are you in the position you want to be?
- Are you worried about having enough money later in life?
- Do you partake in activities that you actually enjoy?
- Does lack of money hold you back from your passions in life?
- Do you think you are spending your money in the correct ways?
- Do you have a plan for your financial future?
- Are you saving enough?
- Do you love the life you are currently living?
- Do you want to have financial freedom?
- Will you ever have financial freedom?

Dangerous, but not scary: Not doing what you love today, spending money on things that don't enrich your life and borrowing from your future without a financial plan in place. This is dangerous but not scary because the status quo is a place of comfort. You don't have any money saved, but most people don't, right? You think you can make up for it at some point in your life. Perhaps it will be when you start to make more money, which is also when you can travel the world and do all the things you desire today.

Credit card and auto loan debt is the normal way of life, right? Seems like the future will "fix" your financial situation, your money habits, and your life. But how? Living without a plan to accomplish your goals is not scary, but oh my, it is dangerous. This is the life you are used to living. You survive just fine each day; things will all come together at some point, right? What if they don't?

The Danger of a "No-Plan" Mindset

You look back at your life at age sixty-five and say, "Wow, I wished I planned more." You realize the mentality of "My future will handle itself without a plan" has finally caught up with you, but it's too late. Turns out your bad habits of purchasing everything on debt never fixed itself; in fact, you may have even taken on even more debt. Turns out that paying for all those useless items with money you never had kept you from spending money on what you actually wanted...your passions in life. Your dream of traveling the world that always seemed to exist five years ahead of you? Five years ahead never happened, and now at retirement age, you don't have the financial freedom you always thought you would. You finally understand that these things don't happen overnight and will never happen for you. That is risk; that is dangerous.

Are you currently living paycheck to paycheck? What would happen if you lost your job? Let that sink in for a few minutes. How would you or your family survive? Would you have to jump into a job you disliked to make ends meet? You need to get in control of your financial situation so that your finances don't control your decisions. Don't let your money or lack thereof make those decisions for you.

I want you to be able to make the correct decisions so an unfortunate money situation will not force your hand. It's not fun to think about worst-case scenarios, but it is necessary in order to get your finances in shape so you will never have to worry. Tough times will come, and money will go up and down, but you don't want your lifestyle to do the same.

Albert Einstein is credited with saying, "The definition of insanity is doing the same thing over and over again, but expecting different results." If you do nothing about your current situation, you will always have the same result. You cannot live on hope with no real plans for the future. You need to get away from saying things like: "I hope I can save more next year," "I hope my car doesn't break down," "I hope I get that raise," etc. While I don't want to be the bearer of bad news, I think you already know that you will never be able to "hope" things into existence.

Going with Your Gut Feeling

One thing often overlooked in life is the benefit of "going with your gut feeling" to make a decision. If you are a smoker, your gut feeling probably tells you to quit on a daily basis. That same gut could tell you that you need to start eating healthier and get to the gym. Your gut would also tell you that you need to change the trajectory of your financial world; change your spending habits and think about the future. The enemy of your gut feelings is your brain, however. Your brain can convince you to do anything if you think about it long enough. You brain will tell you that you can quit later when the time is right. You will start hitting the gym next year as a resolution, and you will save more money when you get that bonus. Don't assume your brain is always looking out for your best interests because it is operating from a state of what is known and what is comfortable.

If your gut is telling you something, listen. Change might happen when it's too late, so don't let that be your story. Focus on the negative impacts if you *don't* change. For smokers, finding the negative impacts are easy: research some medical statistics and envision yourself in the hospital, leaving your friends and family behind at an early age. Food is the same: if you stay on an unhealthy nutritional path, your quality of life will start to deteriorate at an early age. And financially: some day you will no longer be at the peak of your career. Some day when you are older, it will be harder to get a job; the younger generations will have the training it takes to be successful in the workplace. At that point, you may run out of options and either have to take a minimum-wage job behind a cash register or manage on Social Security for the rest of your life. Is your gut telling you that you should start contributing to your 401(k) now? Is it saying you don't need those clothes in your Nordstrom online shopping cart? Your gut is right.

Your Life in Ten Years

Do you want freedom? Do you want control? Do you want the ability to not have to work one day? Then listen to your gut and take action. All I'm asking is that you give up the things that don't add value to your life.

Dream a little bit... What do you envision your life looking like in ten years? What did you imagine yourself looking like ten years ago? Is your current situation different than what you thought it would be back then? Is the person you wanted to be ten years ago different from who you are today? If you failed to become the person you wanted to be ten years ago, how do you plan to become the person you want to be ten years from now? The only way to make this dream a reality is to have an action plan for success and then follow it.

Don't overestimate the future without short-term goals. *Nothing happens in the future; everything is happening now.* Point yourself in the direction you want to go and just start walking. Day by day, week by week, you will see the progress. There will be days that are tougher than others, but just keep walking. Doing so over ten years will lead you to become the person you pictured. Goals are great, and you always want to push yourself to be better. But a large goal that you intend to achieve in ten years is impossible without a plan. Think about walking up stairs. You are not suddenly going to leap up to the top of the staircase. You will take one step at a time. These steps represent the short-term goals that lead to long-term success.

CHAPTER 3

Why Society Struggles with Personal Finance

Monthly payment syndrome (noun): The habit of buying everything on credit, only looking at what something costs you every month instead of what it costs you in total.

The monthly payment syndrome is a sickness that has been sweeping the nation ever since people could borrow money. People tend to overestimate the future. Since you don't have to pay for something right now, your future self is seen as better willing and able to pay for it later. People have no problem committing to something, as long as they don't have to pay for it now. But why?

The Buy-Now, Pay-Later Mentality, aka the Monthly Payment Syndrome

The future is impossible to envision, so your brain creates the output it wants. Your mind can easily convince you that what you are doing now makes sense. Your mind will overestimate how much money you will have in the future, your willingness to reduce debt, and how you will feel about having that debt.

33

The longer you delay payment and take on debt, the more comfortable you'll feel about it and the more your brain will rationalize it. Because of your habits, your brain is wired to disregard the negative outcome of a poor financial decision; it's much more likely to fill your thoughts with that shiny new vehicle you are looking to finance. Your brain will say, "*I can afford $400 a month, and I really want this car; it won't affect me at all in the future. This time it will be different because I'm making more money.*"

But how do you feel about your previous financing decisions? Did the positive feelings surrounding your purchase fade away? Think back to a debt that you are currently trying to pay off. You felt excited when you signed the loan documents and you convinced yourself it was a good decision. How do you feel now that "later" has arrived, and you have to pay for this purchase every month? Your future self is always going to be upset that you took on debt. If you don't want to pay for it now, why would you want to pay for it later?

This buy-now, pay-later mentality is a nasty cycle. The diagnosis is monthly payment syndrome. Once you're in, it's hard to break, and this illness limits your future freedom.

Calculate the Real Cost of Your Purchases

In the world we live in today, most people don't care about the actual cost of things. All they care about is the monthly cost. Break that train of thought and stop thinking this way because what matters most is the total "all in" cost. The whole pay-by-the-month epidemic is a huge marketing scheme that companies use to roll extra hidden costs into products (think interest, financing fees, etc.). They give you a longer time to pay the money back, so it costs you less every month. But the overall cost of the product has *increased* due to all the hidden costs. The amount of your monthly payment is the wrong way to gauge how much the product is costing you.

The longer the term of a loan (i.e. number of years), the lower your monthly payment will be, which is common sense. If I owe the bank $100 over two years, it will cost me $4.16 a month. If I were to pay the bank back over three years, it would cost me $2.77 a month. Why not just pay the bank back over a longer period of time? Two reasons. First, the longer you have to pay for something, the more interest you will pay. This is simple: interest accrues each month, so more months equal more interest. Second, the longer the time you have to pay back the debt, the higher the interest rate you'll be charged. Believe me, companies don't extend longer-term financing because they love their customers; they do it to prey on those who don't understand these financial instruments and will always sign up for a lower monthly payment. Rather than three years, they will give you five, which lowers the payment, but also means they can charge you more interest and collect other fees off the product.

Companies never advertise the total cost of something anymore; they only advertise the monthly payment. Ever see a car commercial? The advertisements always say something like, "Zero down at signing, only $300 monthly!" No total price is ever advertised.

Looking at the world through the lens of a monthly payment makes no financial sense; you will always end up paying more than if you just paid for something upfront. You are buying the same thing, why do you want to pay more for it?

If you cannot afford to pay cash for something, you cannot afford it.

Monthly payment syndrome has now hit epidemic levels. According to CNBC, "The average American now has about $38,000 in personal debt, excluding home mortgages."[8] Based on an *American Banker* article, this is the highest level of debt Americans have ever had.[9] The reason household debt keeps increasing is due to the availability of financing on nearly everything, which lets people delay payment until a later date. The problem is that the consumers end up paying more and the corporations get more of your hard-earned cash.

---

[8] https://www.cnbc.com/2018/08/20/how-much-debt-americans-have-at-every-age.html.

[9] Alan Kline, "Household debt hit another all-time high. Is it poised to level off?" *American Banker*, February 19, 2019, https://www.americanbanker.com/list/household-debt-hit-another-all-time-high-is-it-poised-to-level-off.

This is why you see commercials offering $0 down payment, $0 due at signing, $0 first month payment. Just sign a few pages of paperwork, and the car is yours! Fact check: the car is *not* yours, but the liability sure is. People seem more than fine with stacking liabilities on their future selves: *It's the future so I will just deal with it then*. As long as they don't have to pay for it now, they will sign on the dotted line. Does putting something off really make it better? Think about mowing the grass for example. Do you ever think to yourself, *I'm so happy I waited to mow my lawn, I can think of nothing more I wanted to do at this very moment, my past-self sure was correct*?

Ask yourself: If I don't want to pay for something right now, why would I want to pay more for the same thing later? To any rational person that takes time to think about it, that makes absolutely no sense. Let me reiterate the concept: you don't want to pay for it now, but you are okay with paying even *more* for the *same* thing later. That still makes no sense to me. Since money is hard to earn and hard to keep, you should strive to get deals on all purchases, not pay more. Don't burden your future with payment procrastination.

The Rise of Debt, the Common Enemy

We all have a common enemy and its name is *debt*. In today's world, it is all too easy to access. You can finance cars, wedding rings, golf clubs, furniture, tires... the list goes on. The fact that you can finance pretty much anything is changing our purchasing behavior, and we don't even realize it.

Did you know that the word "freedom" actually originates from a term meaning free from debt? Quick fact: debt has been used for centuries and has continually created massive problems for society. In the olden days, if you could not pay back your loans, the moneylenders would seize your land, livestock, and even family members (including wives and children) as repayment of the debt. This led people who were in financial trouble to flee the cities in which they lived to avoid having their family members taken away. As all the workers fled the villages, the government realized they would need to grant forgiveness for the debts owed, or the economy would not survive. If you don't have people to work, you won't have an economy. This is where the word freedom was born, when the villagers were freed from their debts.[10]

Let's take another step back in time to look at the history of some of the popular debt products we have today.

Car Loans

Car loans began as an instrument to help the greater population purchase cars. An individual would be required to put 35% down, and the loan was only for a twelve-month period. This sounds crazy, and if we had this today, a lot of people would be walking to work. During that time, wealthy people were the only ones who had access to the automobile market, so banks, preying on peoples' wants, gave a path to ownership for the middle class. Instant gratification was born. This love for instant gratification got so bad that people would take extremely high interest rate loans in order to own that dream car. Consumerism at its finest. The government even had to step in at one point to regulate car loans to prevent predatory lending practices.

This was a factor in the Great Depression. Instant gratification is never a sustainable practice. The banks started lending out too much from customer deposits and neglected to maintain adequate cash reserves. This works, until people want to withdraw their money. Because the banks didn't have adequate reserves, they could not provide cash withdrawals to customers. This caused a domino effect, because people started rushing the banks in fear of losing all their money. When banks can no longer give you the money in your account, people tend to freak out. That is exactly what happened in 1929 due to nonexistent banking regulations. Does this sound familiar? Think back to 2008: same problem, different asset (the housing market).

To recap, car loans originally had a one-year term; now you can finance a car for seven years. Companies figured out that by stretching out the terms

[10] David Graeber, "9 Things You Didn't Know About the History of Debt," *The Huffington Post,* July 29, 2011, https://www.huffingtonpost.com/david-graeber/history-debt_b_913419.html?slideshow=true#gallery/5bb640f5e4b039c2956c0963/2.

on a loan, the monthly payment goes down. When the payment each month is lower, the demand rises. They are changing consumer behavior and the way we think about money. A low monthly payment is nice, but it really means you are paying *more* interest over a *longer* period of time. It seems that nobody cares about that; they are only concerned about a low monthly payment, and getting what they want now. This is the root cause of monthly payment syndrome.

I bet car advertisements back in the day simply listed the car prices. Now car commercials give stupid, meaningless numbers like $416. No, the total cost is not $416; that's the monthly payment. That $416 is full of interest expense and extra fees. Wake up people, and stop using expensive debt products for instant gratification.

Mortgage Loans

Think about a house. If you own one, you probably have a thirty-year mortgage. The term length of a mortgage used to be just five years. Over time, the terms have stretched out further and further to what we have today. The banks increased the length of the loans, so borrowers would have a lower monthly payment, but they also pay much more in interest. There's a common theme here.

This "standard" is a perfect scenario for banks. They generate more revenue from the interest on the loans and since the monthly payment is lower, the demand for the product skyrockets. While it is nice to have a thirty-year loan, you will pay significantly more for your house over those thirty years than if you paid it off earlier. Interest expense on a thirty-year mortgage will cost nearly the price of the home. Yes, that is right; you could pay double for your home. If you are buying a $300,000 home, you will pay nearly $300,000 in interest expense, depending on your interest rate.

It is understandable borrowing money for a home, but borrowing from the banks has now been taken to a whole new level. You can finance anything today, which feeds the monthly payment syndrome illness in this country.

Household debt has now gone past 2008 recession levels, driven primarily by student and auto loans. Let that sink in...it's an alarming statistic. However, consumers are not the only ones acquiring debt at massive rates. Our government has also incurred immense amounts of debt. Did you know that every U.S. citizen would have to pay about $67,000 in order to pay off the U.S. debt at this time? That statistic includes those who don't pay taxes (i.e., children). If we start talking taxpayers only, then every taxpayer would have to pay approximately $179,000 to pay off the government's debt right now.[11]

The fifth largest budget item for the U.S. government is servicing the country's debt (paying interest on loans). At this time, interest expense costs the U.S. government $343 billion a year, or over $1,100 for each U.S. citizen. [12] That is right: even if you are debt free at the moment, some of your money from every paycheck is paying for the country's debt. Can you believe that? WOW, I think we could be spending our money in a much more productive fashion.

Unfortunately, Personal Finance is not Taught in School

This is one of my biggest pet peeves because personal finance plays such a big role in everyone's life. In high school, we learn how to do geometry and even have cooking classes. When we graduate and go to college and take astronomy, philosophy, and sociology classes. I'm not being dramatic; I took all those classes in my educational career. To be honest, I never liked these classes, and always had a hard time paying attention because I could not apply them to my life. I'm glad we're taught how to prove that two triangles are congruent, but when was the last time that helped you do your taxes, understand your loan terms, or the difference between a Roth 401(k) and a traditional 401(k)? Wouldn't it be much more helpful to study the real-world

---

[11] http://www.usdebtclock.org/, December 14, 2018.

[12] Ibid.

financial situations we all encounter throughout our lives? Couldn't we at least learn about student loan debt and how to pay it off after college?

Too many people get into credit card and student loan debt during their college years. This is because the average college student is not educated on the long-term impacts of debt, so it's not seen as a big deal. Really, it's viewed as free money: *The bank wouldn't give me this money if I didn't deserve it.* The fact that the government and financial institutions can profit on debt instruments extended to young adults who have never learned about them seems pretty messed up to me. What many young adults don't realize is that if you don't pay them back on time, they will ruin your credit score. Plus, having large debt when you start out will limit your ability to buy a home or get any other sort of financing in the future.

I have a huge problem with this, which is why I'm a walking billboard with a megaphone for learning about personal finance. It's never too early or too late to learn how to manage your personal finances. When I hear anyone talking about a financial issue, I quickly swoop in and break it down into terms people understand if they ask my opinion. It's very rewarding to try to help people improve their financial decision-making skills. I love seeing the light bulb illuminate when they finally understand an issue, know how to solve it, and put my advice into action to maximize their life and money.

My favorite part about helping people is when I see them again and they tell me what they are doing to increase their net worth. They might say, "Cory, we paid off all our credit card cards and we don't feel so burdened. We are so much happier now!" "Cory, we saved up enough money and now we are closing on a house." Or, "Cory, since talking to you, we consolidated all our debt into a low rate and will have it paid off soon." This is awesome, and I love helping people see the light and change how they attack life and money. They end up healthier, both financially and mentally.

I would like to see all schools incorporate the following personal finance basics into their curriculums:

- What is a savings account?
- What is a retirement account?
- How do you balance a checkbook?
- How credit cards work?

- What is a credit score?
- How do debit cards work?
- What is compound interest and how does it work?
- How do I calculate net worth?
- How do loans work?
- Why is saving at a young age important?
- What is a W2 and how do I complete my taxes?

Since the school system has failed on the topic of personal finance, we rely on examples in our personal lives to learn the basics. Unfortunately, not everyone has great examples of personal finance practices in their lives.[13] As mentioned earlier, the average American household has around $38,000 in consumer debt. I'm not sure that average Americans are the best people to give advice about how to structure your life and money. It is alarming to see people's lives take a turn for the worse due to money problems that are 100% avoidable through education.

Once the vicious cycle of debt commences, it controls your life, and you begin to focus on the wrong things. My goal with this book is to enrich everyone's lives and have them realize that financial freedom is something everyone can achieve regardless of where you are in life. Being able to better people's lives is very rewarding for me.

---

[13] https://www.nerdwallet.com/blog/average-credit-card-debt-household/.

CHAPTER 4

Living Your Dream Life While Conquering Your Financial Goals

The main reason I make working out and staying in shape a priority is so I can do all the active things I love without being exhausted. I don't think an out-of-shape person would enjoy a 3,500 foot vertical climb up a trail on a mountain bike. Being in shape gives me the ability to enjoy things like that. Similarly, being financially fit gives me the ability to live the life I want and love the life I live. Financially fit people do everything they want to in life and accomplish personal financial goals in the process, all while sticking to a budget.

I always tell people to think back to what they spent money on last month or last year. Next, think about what you spent money on last month or last year that actually brought you joy, warmed your heart, or triggers happy memories. Can you even remember what you bought? Not easy, is it? Maybe you are spending money on the wrong things. Money is not easy to make and is even harder to keep. Why would you spend it on things that are not bringing you joy or enriching your life?

A financially fit person is on autopilot when it comes to spending because their wallet, heart, and mind are aligned to value. There is an evolution to be becoming financially fit just like there is an evolution to becoming physically fit. It's basically the same formula of building a habit and tracking it against a plan. Being physically fit is a balance; humans are hardwired to enjoy eating foods that are not necessarily good for them because they taste amazing. However, if it's important for you to get physically fit, you will need to control what you eat, find foods that you love that are still good for you, and make sure you exercise properly for your goals. Before you know it, you will seek out the food that tastes good, but is also healthy. You will fall in love with exercising due to the released endorphins. You will find a way to afford the calories of a "cheat meal," but only occasionally, and only when it's worth it. That is a healthy balance, which is only achieved by a change in habits; you now experienced that the initial transformation was the only hard part...maintaining is easier. Once this becomes the norm, you will feel odd *not* living in this manner.

You will learn that in order to maintain, you cannot just cut everything out of our life that is "bad" for you. You love the pizza and ice cream every once in a while, so it's also important to find a balance and enjoy the foods you really love because you cannot have them all the time. If you know you are going out for pizza and beer tonight, you may work out and eat really healthy during the day so you can "afford" the calories that night. Life is all about balance. Now think about everything you just read and relate it to money. It's the same concept.

Your Financial Life in Balance

If you want to become financially fit you need to live it on a daily basis for at least three weeks. After three weeks, a habit will start to form, and you will suddenly feel enlightened by your new state of mind. It soon becomes a passion to stay financially fit, and you will understand that the transformation is the hardest phase; maintaining is the easier part. You will come to learn the balance. You cannot just cut everything out of your life and never spend a dollar; you love certain things in life, so in finding balance, you will only spend on things or experiences you love and are passionate about because you know money is a precious commodity.

Financially fit people do everything they want to in life and accomplish personal financial goals in the process, all while sticking to a budget. In order to become financially fit, look inside yourself and think in the long term without any distractions. Answer these two questions:

1. What actually makes me happy?
2. What is the best dollar I spent last month?

It is important to direct your money into purchases that give you the highest happiness return on investment (ROI). Before you know it, you will only be spending money on items that *enrich* your life. It might shock you, but it will be a relatively small number of things that actually add value to your life. When you cut out the random purchases that have no impact, you will start to feel as if you are spending more since you are only spending on the items and experiences you will remember and cherish. This mindset will help you chase what you love and increase your overall happiness.

How you might ask? Each minute of every day you need to focus on bringing value to your life and ignoring anything that is not a positive benefit for you.

For example, my wife and I have seen very little changes to our spending budget over the past five years. Yes, we make more money now than we did five years ago, but why would we change our spending habits if we already love our life inside the walls of our budget? Having a budget early on made us focus on what to prioritize in life. Since it was of great importance to us to stick to our budget, we quickly realized what brought absolutely zero value to our life, cut it out, and reallocated our assets to what does bring value. Yes, this practice increases your savings, but, most importantly, it increases your enjoyment.

Budgeting

Since a budget is a set amount of money, you can only spend that amount to follow it. I have learned to get creative to acquire what I want. I find discounts on things because I don't want to discount my life. Creating a budget and sticking to it may feel hard at first, but once you practice it for a couple weeks and then a couple months, you won't even need to look at your budget. You will have learned to operate in that realm without needing to remind yourself. All the while, your life enjoyment has increased because you are now laser-focused on what truly makes you happy, what is actually valuable to you

This mentality is addictive because you will see your money consistently grow while living the life you love. If you ever have to say no to something because of money, sit down that night and strategize about how to do it for less and where you can allocate savings from other areas.

Remember when I was younger and would sleep in the lobby so that I could ski? I'm not saying to go to that extreme, but you will learn to get creative in order to do the things you value. To find value in every situation, ask yourself:

- Why am I doing this?
- What do I love about this experience?
- What specifically is valuable about it?
- What am I going to remember about this experience?

You'll need to uncover the answers, which are the keys to being financially fit. For example, we love to travel, but the flight is not the highlight of our trip. We find ways to get free flights, such as using travel miles. If you want to spend a week in Rome, make yourself breakfast and coffee every day instead of going to Starbucks so you can save enough to take your dream trip. Life is all about balance; find what drives you and eliminate the rest.

Think in the Long Term, but Focus on the Short Term

Hitting daily, weekly, monthly, and yearly budget goals is, by far, the most important practice in personal financial management. We know Rome was not built in a day. We know each daily win adds to a weekly win, which adds to a monthly win ... well, you get the picture. The short term should be your focus, though, because without execution in the short term, you won't be able to realize the long-term benefits. My eyes are fixed on the future, but I have a magnifying glass on the present. If I stick to my plan in each day, I know where I will be financially next month, next year, and five years from now... ultimately having financial freedom.

Agree to Take Action

History is the best indicator of the future. If you keep doing what you are doing, you will end up in the same spot you are today. Are you sick of *not* living the life you've always envisioned? Stop letting money control you. Get in control of your money.

You want to be financially fit. But how are you going to get there? How are you going to pay off your car later if you don't want to begin paying it off now? Stop making excuses, and be real with yourself. Change your behavior now in order to impact your future.

Just like getting to the top of a staircase, you need to commit to taking the first step in order to climb the remaining steps. The first step is the most important one. Committing to take action to reach your small goals is the gateway to your dreams. You are not suddenly going to have $1 million, and you are not suddenly going to become debt free. How do you get to your end goal? You can make your choice today and take small steps each day. That decision, and your small steps in the present, are the keys to building wealth and becoming financially fit. Live in the present: One million dollars in the future represents one million decisions and actions that happen in the present. Action in the present will create the future you dream about.

Stop being a victim to your thoughts and current habits. Have you ever looked back in your life and wish you saved less? No. Have you ever looked back and wished you had made more impulse purchases? No.

Take a stand right now. Admit to yourself that you are not where you want to be. This is great, that is the first step. Commit to making a change, and make that agreement with yourself. The situation you are in financially right now does not have to be permanent, and you just made a commitment to change. This is a big deal, congratulations! You are on the road to becoming financially fit. Your biggest asset is time, and there is no time like right now.

The first step toward taking appropriate action is creating your financial road map; a budget.

CHAPTER 5

The Only Budget You Will Ever Need

You might be thinking, "Oh *man, here comes the boring stuff: budgets."* Try thinking about it differently. A budget doesn't have to be boring, and it will truly enhance your life. Remember that a budget is not a limitation or restriction; a budget is a maximization of your resources. Why does the word "budget" come with such a negative connotation?

Who Has a Budget?

Budget is a word typically associated with people who are struggling to make ends meet. Those people *need* to budget for every dollar because their resources are scarce. Break this perception because a budget is a tool for people who want to become wealthy and stay that way. Non-wealthy people should budget, but they typically don't, while wealthy people do budget in order to maximize every dollar they make.

Building a successful budget is based on understanding your behavior and your lifestyle, then creating a balanced plan to help you accomplish what you enjoy *and* reach your financial goals. What do you think every company does before any business is transacted, before any employees are hired, and before any project is approved? They create a budget about four months before the year starts. Companies will spend those four months running through countless iterations until they finalize the official financial plan (i.e. budget) for the following year. Would you invest in a company without a financial plan? Financial planning is one of the most important functions for a business. The financial plan lays the groundwork for how the business will operate.

Do businesses track results against their budgets? The answer is: Yes. Large companies hire teams of talented finance and accounting professionals to track every dollar earned and spent, down to the penny. Once all dollars are accounted for, management is tasked with explaining the variances against the budget to shareholders of the business. They analyze what is working, what is not working, where they can squeeze out more savings, and where they can invest more for the highest returns. Management will do everything they can to meet or exceed the budget because their annual bonus is benchmarked off those results. It's time to start viewing your personal financial world like a corporation, because your life is your own personal business.

If that sounds impossible, I guarantee you it's not. We will walk through the process step by step, and there are free templates for you to download on our website; thirtysomethingmillionaire.com. I will show you how to build a budget that you can stick to, no excuses. If you have ever had trouble staying on track with a budget, you were going about building it incorrectly. You'll need flexibility, and I will show you how to assess your financial world to maximize your personal resources. Think about the stress that will be removed when you understand exactly where you will be, money-wise, at the end of the year, and which targets you need to hit each day/week/month to get there.

A budget is a tool to *spend to*, not to *spend under*. This may sound different from your prior definition of a budget. Having a budget will force you to choose ahead of time what you enjoy versus what you dislike. This principle is very valuable. This is the key is sticking to your plan, no matter what. Going through life without a plan is stressful. Grab the wheel of your finances, stop being a passenger, and create a GPS for your money to maximize your resources and your life.

Perks of Having a Budget

Think of a budget as a trail map to your ultimate destination: a spending roadmap, if you will. When you go on a hike for the first time, do you look at a trail map or do you just wander around the woods, *hoping* to reach your final destination? When you head to a new spot for dinner, do you enter the address into your phone for directions, or do you just wing it and hope you will get there? Similar to how you use your GPS for directions, a budget is the GPS to your financial goals. Think about how you manage your money and ask yourself the following questions:

Do you have a roadmap to achieve your goals?

How do you know where you will be at the end of the year?

How much can you spend each month to ensure you are still saving enough?

- What are your financial goals?
- How are you tracking compared to those goals?
- How do you know if you will have enough money when you retire?
- Do you ever stress about money?

Why would you go through life without a financial plan to maximize one of the most important items (money) in your life?

People often turn a blind eye to having financial goals. This can stem from feeling like their goals are out of reach or from a future mindset of thinking it will "just happen." Like when you "have more money," or "it's just impossible to save now." Saying to yourself, "I will have a nice house, a nice car, and a fat savings account later when I'm rich." Again, I ask, how are you going to do this? What is your plan? How will you get that nice house, car, and savings account? If you don't have your financial GPS turned on, how will you arrive at that destination?

The Seven-Step Guide to the Only Budget You Will Ever Need

A budget is not a limitation to save; it's a road map of what you can *spend* to reach your chosen destination.

"If you fail to plan, you are planning to fail."

—Benjamin Franklin

How do you come up with a financially fit plan? How do you get out of debt? How do you plan for the largest purchases in your life? Becoming financially fit is a total transformation to your current lifestyle and will produce life-changing results!

I'm about to walk you through how to create an individualized plan that works with your lifestyle, income and goals. Your plan has to be successful for *you*. It all comes down to what you enjoy and value. I will help you discover what you value so you can maximize your money and save the rest. Easy concept, right? The goal is to find balance. If you put yourself on too strict of a plan, you will fail because you won't be doing the things you consider fun. That approach will lead to resentment of your financial plan and budgeting in general. If you have a realistic approach that allows you to still enjoy your life, you will feel empowered about your choices and will continuously be excited when you keep achieving your goals.

If this is your first time building a budget, this might seem like a very large task. Don't worry, we will attack it in bite-sized steps. What we are about to build is called a cash flow statement, or a profit and loss statement, as corporations call it. At the end of the day, the goal is to "forecast" how much money will be in your bank account at certain points of time in the future.

Money is one of the most important aspects of your life. Investing the time to create your plan is well worth it. You spend eight hours or more, five or more days a week earning money. It makes complete sense to sit down and budget for how you want to maximize it, considering all the hours you worked to earn a paycheck.

Before we get started, take a step right now to create a time on your calendar to update your budget each week. Plan to spend around thirty minutes for this activity.

I will wait… Block thirty minutes on your calendar now; occurring each week, same time, no end date.

I do this first thing Monday morning. Every week, the first thing I do is sit down and update my budget. This includes categorizing each dollar I spent the week before and updating any future budget months based on my historical spending. Of any habit you create, this is the most important one, so schedule that time in your calendar now before you read another word.

Step 1: Build Your Template

Building a budget in Excel or Google Sheets does not take a lot of expertise, and you don't need to use a sophisticated statistical forecasting model.

Let's first talk about the correct way to build a budget. The way I think about a budget is top to bottom—beginning with the needs and working your way down to the wants. The following budget example will serve as a guide to help you understand how to build your own. Head over to thirtysomething-millionaire.com to download your free template.

Personal Budget

	Jan	----->	Dec	Year
Income & Savings				
Income (After Tax)	$		$	$
Bonus (After Tax)	$		$	$
Minus 15% Savings	$		$	$
(1) Income After Taxes and Savings	$		$	$
Housing Expenses				
Rent / Mortgage	($)		($)	($)
Utilities	($)		($)	($)
(2) Total Housing Expenses	($)		($)	($)
Living expenses				
Grocery Store	($)		($)	($)
Gasoline Expenses	($)		($)	($)
Car Insurance	($)		($)	($)
Cable, Internet, Cell Phone	($)		($)	($)
(3) Total Living Expenses	($)		($)	($)
Other				
Budget Breakers	($)		($)	($)
Gym Membership	($)		($)	($)
SLUSH Fund	($)		($)	($)
His / Her Quarterly Ration	($)		($)	($)
Travel & Other	($)		($)	($)
(4) Total Other Expense	($)		($)	($)
Debt (Excluding Mortgage)				
Auto Loan	($)		($)	($)
Student Loan	($)		($)	($)
(5) Total Debt payments	($)		($)	($)
Prior Month Cash Balance	$		$	$
+ Cash Flow = +1 MINUS (2+3+4+5)	$		$	$
= Cash Balance	$		$	$

At a high level, start with your income and then subtract your living and entertainment expenses, which will leave you with your net income. There are a lot of great tools today for budgeting, but I believe automated tools prohibit full ownership of your financial world. Manually updating your budget helps you understand your financial world. It's a bit more time consuming, but you will be able to track every dollar spent, correctly categorize it, and understand it as well. I find this is the only way for me and my clients to understand what is actually being spent. It's much more painful to document every source of overspending and have to reduce other spending to hit your savings targets. You will start to really understand your financial world by manually tracking everything that comes in and goes out.

On the flip side, it's also more rewarding to record savings to your budget and increase your spending for that Paris trip later this year. You can be much more creative when you have a budget that can easily be updated in a spreadsheet. As I mentioned previously, I start off every Monday morning by updating my budget. Once you are in the habit of updating your budget weekly, you will master the art of value spending, and your savings and life enjoyment will increase. The initial period of change is the only obstacle. Remember that once you create a new habit, that habit is the new normal.

Your budget should be weekly because it's the best way to get a grip on spending. If you try to analyze a months' worth of spending, you will find that the amount of data will be overwhelming and hard to dissect. Also, breaking bad spending habits will be harder because your financial reviews are spread too far apart. A lot can happen in a month. Keep a pulse on your money by reviewing each week, that way you can track progress, and quickly break bad spending habits and learn to maximize your life and money. If you downloaded the template you will notice its set up for weekly input and updating.

Step 2: Data

Before you start inputting numbers into your fancy new template, collect a few months of recent financial statements to get an understanding of your entire financial picture. Save this information to a folder or print the following:

- Bank statements (checking, savings, etc).
- Pay stubs.
- Credit or debit card statements.
- All loans: mortgage, auto, student, everything.
- Other: any other products/instruments you use to spend or save money.

Step 3: Calculate Take-Home Pay

Let's take it from the top, starting with income.

Income after taxes and savings

Determine your take-home pay. Take-home pay = Gross income *minus* Taxes *minus* Savings. Pay your taxes first, pay yourself second (savings), then budget your spending with what's left over. We are looking to understand how much money will be deposited into your bank account each payday.

1: Taxes

If you work for a company, your taxes are most likely taken out of your paycheck before you receive it. If you are self-employed, you will need to estimate and pay your taxes on a quarterly basis. To ensure you have money set aside for taxes, create a savings account and have the appropriate percentage of your income automatically deposited into this account, which will function as an escrow account for your tax liability. This money is not, and never was yours, so don't even think about spending it.

2: Savings

Your savings goal should be 15% of your gross income, which is what you make before taxes are taken out. I like to think of savings as a tax you pay to yourself. The government gets a cut of your income and so should you. A savings goal of at least 15% will put you in a fantastic position later in life, and provide that financial freedom you desire.

The 15% "savings waterfall": I like to think about savings as a waterfall that has three pools.

Pool #1: The first pool to fill up is *debt reduction*. If you have any debt (we are excluding a mortgage here), paying it off is your top priority. If you are debt free, excluding a mortgage, this pool is full, so feel free to skip down to Pool #2. Before any of your savings can go toward building up your three to six months of safety net savings or investing, you first need to save $1,000-$2,000 for an emergency fund, then use every extra dollar you save to pay off your debts (excluding your mortgage). Once this pool is full (debt free, excluding mortgage), the water (15% of savings) will overflow into the next pool.

If you are heavy in debt or in dire straits financially, I recommend reading *The Total Money Makeover* by Dave Ramsey.[14] Although I don't agree with many of the limitations he puts on his readers, he does have a great system for debt reduction.

Later in the book we will go into detail on the best way to start attacking your debt. I call it the "Debt Diet Plan." How much money you need to direct towards paying off debt will depend on the severity of your debt situation. This is not a one-size-fits-all situation. If you are in debt, *at least* 15% of your take-home pay needs to go toward paying it down. Attacking your debt is your top priority.

Pool #2: Three to six months of *safety net savings*. Once you are debt free (give yourself a pat on the back first) you need to build up a safety net to guard you and your family (if you have one) from financial hardship. You already knocked out the most dangerous financial threat, which is debt. Now

[14] Dave Ramsey, *The Total Money Makeover* (Nashville, TN: Nelson Books, 2013).

you need to use that 15% of your income to fortify the walls around your financial world. Take a look at your total monthly expenses and multiply that number by a range of three to six. This is the target balance of cash you need sitting in an account that you don't touch that will act as a safety net if something goes wrong (think losing a job, medical bills, car bills, house bills...the list goes on). Should you save three or six months of expenses? That depends on your situation. If you have a family or have a single income I would lean towards six months. If you and your partner are DINKs (dual income and no kids), then you might not need six months of savings.

All too often I talk to people who are chomping at the bit to invest every dollar they make. In order to invest one dollar, you must have zero debt (excluding a mortgage), and three to six months of savings in cash inside of a savings account that you don't touch. If you invest money, you should not plan to touch this money for a long time. Therefore, every dollar invested will be locked up. You must have a safety net of cash for emergencies first, before you have the ability to lock money up in an investment. The last thing you want with investments is to have to withdraw from them early, which might involve extra fees or selling at a loss during a downturn in the market. The second pool to fill up with your 15% of savings is three to six months of safety net savings. Once this pool is full, the water will overflow into the next pool.

Pool #3: – Investments. This final pool has no maximum capacity. The other two pools need to be full before you start investing any extra money. Stash away 15% of your gross income in your 401(k), IRA, or a savings account. Important reminder: I'm not an investment professional, I'm a do-more-with-less professional, and before you invest your money, always consult an expert.

The point here: is you will always be saving 15% of your money, no matter what.

Do I need to show the money going into savings or other accounts in my budget? If you asked this question, give yourself a pat on the back. Right now we are building a *cash spending budget*, and retirement or savings accounts will be captured on your balance sheet. At this point, we only care about the cash going into your personal bank account that you can spend. We are not looking at the amount you have in savings at this time; that comes later.

Do you have any other forms of income: any side hustles? Bonus? Wage increases? Whatever it is, give it a low estimate, give it a date, and input that amount. Think about all types of income and include them in your budget.

Step 4: Itemizing Your Expenses (the Needs)

Housing expenses: Everything related to keeping a roof over your head. You should have some of the following monthly expense lines in your budget:

- Rent or mortgage,
- HOA dues,
- Property taxes,
- Homeowners or renters insurance,
- Utilities (water, heat, air conditioning, electricity, etc.),
- Cable, Netflix,
- Internet, home phone, etc.
- If you own a home, you will also need to create a budget for home maintenance.

Oh, the joys that come with home ownership: fixing a door, grass seed, repairing a toilet, furnace filters, etc. A good estimate for this maintenance line is 0.5% to 1% of your home's value. This all depends, obviously. Did you buy a fixer upper home? If so, more money will need to be allocated to this expense line. On the flip side, if you bought a brand-new house, you may need $0. How to figure that out? Check out the historical spending from your bank statement and determine what you have been spending to maintain your home. Okay, it seems like we have a lot of "needs" so far. When do we get to the fun stuff? Don't worry, the "wants" section is coming soon.

Living expenses: We want to capture all other needs you have on a monthly basis. The key word here is *need*. The following are categories nearly everyone has:

Groceries: include anything inside of the walls of a grocery store (this does *not* include eating out; that is a *want,* not a *need*). Food, razors, shampoo, paper towels, alcohol, snacks, etc. Please be careful if you grocery shop at Target, though. Clothes and that cute throw pillow should not be counted in your grocery expense, these are also a want.

- Car-related expenses: gasoline, insurance, and regular maintenance.
- Cell phone.
- Day-care expense.
- Pet medical expenses, such as heartworm and annual checkups.

There are many more, but think about everything you need to survive each month or year aside from what we talked about in the housing expenses section. Finding and forecasting these items should be easy as you probably spend close to the same amount every month on them.

Budget Tip: Overestimate expenses and underestimate income, which is commonly referred to as *sandbagging*. The definition of sandbagging, per the Urban Dictionary, is "to deliberately perform at a lower level then you are capable of." Sandbagging will give your budget some flexibility. Or said another way: budget more than you usually spend. If you usually spend around $100 a week on groceries, then budget $130. If you can continually spend $30 less a week than you budgeted for groceries, as an example, you can shift $30 x 52 weeks in a year = $1,560 into that trip you always wanted to take. I don't want you to save money over what you budgeted in total. I want you to build a budget that you are comfortable sticking to, and if you save in some areas, then you deserve the reward of spending it on your passions.

This concept goes the other way, as well, and it's painful. If you overspend, you need to cut back in other areas. At the end of the year, I want you to be $0.25 under your budget target, then take the $0.25 and buy yourself a gumball; good job. This means you spent exactly to your plan and successfully predicted how much you needed, had fun with your wants, and saved your targeted amount.

Step 5: Budget Breakers

I promise we are getting closer to wants. But before we get to wants, let's set aside some money for what we don't want: things that can break your budget. Car repairs, vet bills, medical bills, etc. Basically, any unexpected big bills = budget breakers. These are unplanned events and are zero fun to deal with. There are two different ways to think about them.

Number 1: *Budget Breakers with three to six months of safety net savings.* Don't budget for them and cross your fingers they don't happen. The reason you have three to six months of savings is for expenses just like these, the unexpected ones. If you are in the privileged position of having adequate savings, you don't need to budget for them. If you do happen to have a budget breaker, pay for it out of these funds, then save 15% of your income after the budget breaker to fill your savings account back up.

Number 2: *Budget Breakers without three to six months of safety net savings.* A good rule of thumb is budgeting $2,000 for items like this. Budget this money early in the year. If you don't have a budget breaker, put that money into an account labeled emergency. You budgeted to spend it, so as long as you stay on your budget you will have the $2,000 left over. That $2,000 can be deposited into an account labeled "emergency." The next year when you budget, input that same $2,000 and don't ever touch the "emergency" account unless you need it. If you don't spend the money that next year, put that toward debt or your three to six months of safety net savings. As long as you have that original $2,000 sitting in an emergency account, you can rest easier at night until you get on your feet financially. The goal here is to make sure those expenses don't have you reaching for your credit card to pay for something and leave you in a situation where you cannot pay off the credit card.

Being prepared not only gives you peace of mind, it will eliminate the possibility of having to go into debt to fix something. Since I have been on the same budget for a long time and my income has increased, I'm at the point where these budget breakers only serve to irritate me because they hurt my net-worth goal for the year. If my income goes up, but my budget is the same, where do you think the money goes? To savings and investments. If I have to bring my savings down to fund something unexpected, that is no big deal. The value of having this security is priceless.

Step 6: Fun Money, the World of Wants

Our first segment into wants! I like to think of wants as luxury expenses that would be the first to go if you needed to cut back on your spending for any reason. Think about anything that was not captured as a "living expense" and put those line items here. There will be another bucket for entertainment, but I want to capture things you pay for on a monthly basis that are not absolutely necessary, such as cable subscriptions, Audible, gym memberships, haircuts, etc. We want to itemize all luxuries in life before getting into entertainment expenses, or what we like to call the SLUSH Fund.

The SLUSH Fund, Spending Account (Wants)

Now this is where the fun(d) starts, and if you only pay attention to one part of the book, this is it: the SLUSH Fund spending account, the flexible spending budget that you can spend in any way you like.

According to Merriam Webster: slush fund (noun): an unregulated fund often used for illicit purposes...Your "illicit" spending is unique to you, whether it's going to Starbucks, buying dog toys, buying drinks for all your friends, or going out to eat. The point here is, you can spend this money on whatever you want. It's impossible to categorize all your spending because it changes so much on a monthly basis. Categorize everything you can; everything else will come out of your SLUSH Fund.

This line item is your *true value identifier*. As you have noticed, I've laid out most of the different categories of monthly expenditures, and they were rather "un-fun." The goal here is to identify all recurring expenses, and the items that are not recurring go in the SLUSH Fund catch-all bucket for the day-to-day random spending (fun money). The SLUSH Fund is the value identifier because it's limited each week. You would be surprised at how far you can stretch this fund. This spending account is what separates the amateurs from the pros, the financially unprepared from the millionaires.

Here is an exercise I want you to complete. How many times each week do you think you make a purchase under $20? Come up with a number, then pull your bank statements from last month and circle all the transactions under $20. Get your calculator out and add them up, then divide by how many weeks in that month and analyze the trend. Shocking, isn't it? I bet the actual number is at least two times higher than the number you thought it was. These smaller transactions are silent wealth killers, and all these little purchases probably have *zero* impact on your life and don't increase your happiness.

You can eliminate most of this spending from your life and never notice it. As I said earlier, I never say *no* to anything because of money. Sometimes I overspend my SLUSH Fund, sometimes I spend under. However, my overall goal is to hit my year-end target, so I try to stay close to my weekly average spending. If you are poor at tracking your weekly spending, try putting cash into your wallet at the start of every week; it will go a lot faster than you think and will force you to get creative on how you spend these funds. I bet you will think twice before you hit Starbucks every day before work. The SLUSH Fund is the most important part of your budget; spend it however you like, but the bucket is limited, so you will be forced to seek value. Being resourceful is the point here.

Budget Tip: How to be financially fit with your SLUSH Fund: Dinner and drinks with friends; a night out on the town.

Going out to eat with friends... I'm not much of a foodie. In fact, I actually benchmark every meal off the price of a Chipotle Burrito Bowl because there is great value in that meal, and it's delicious. At Chipotle, my wife and I split a burrito bowl by ordering a tortilla on the side. I empty my half out into the tortilla and roll a burrito and she grabs a spoon and eats her half of the bowl.

Chipotle tip #1: you can order up to three tortillas on the side for no extra charge.

Chipotle tip #2: you get almost 50% more food if you order a bowl with the tortilla on the side, rather than just ordering a burrito.

A meal that is quick, reasonably healthy, and delicious ends up costing around $8.00 for both of us. I love Chipotle more than the food served at most sit-down restaurants. So when my friends want to eat at some trendy place that charges an insane about of money for a small portion of hipster food, I will just eat Chipotle on the way and enjoy everyone's company while enjoying my full belly and full bank account. After the dinner is done, how about heading to your favorite watering hole with friends?

My key move is to walk up to the bar to order my drinks, even if we are out with friends at a table and have a waiter/waitress serving us. I don't like to get into splitting bills, so to control that I order drinks at the bar. My first question is asking what is on happy hour. If they don't have a happy hour, I ask for the cheapest beer on the menu.

A night out with friends rarely costs my wife and I more than $25 in total, while my friends will be lucky if they spend less than $100 after dinner and drinks. It's not how much money you spend, it's how you use it. And that is just Friday night...

If I spend $75 dollars less every Friday night, that ends up being almost $4,000 a year in savings. I can take a trip to Spain for almost two weeks with that kind of money. At the end of the day, my friends' experiences are not any better than mine. They do seem to be a little jealous when I'm in Spain. Be the person who goes to Spain.

Her and His Quarterly Ration

This line of the budget is the same as the SLUSH Fund account, but it's a completely independent line item for larger wants during the year. The following are those used by my wife and I.

Her Quarterly Ration: My wife can spend this money on whatever she wants. Most of the time she uses the money for shopping, getting her hair, and her nails done. She still will not let me cut her hair, even though *I* think I would do a great job! She can also spend it on concert tickets, a night out with friends, or throw this money out of her window on the highway. You get the point: this is her money to spend on whatever she wants. Now I'm not being sexist here, but women's self-maintenance products and services do cost more than men's. I also understand that beauty products add value to my wife's life because she likes taking care of herself and splurges every once in a while. When I see random charges from a nail salon or from her favorite clothing store, I just ding the Quarterly Ration budget. She often uses this account for clothes, going to brunch with her friends, buying makeup, getting her hair done, or monthly subscriptions like FabFitFun boxes.

We budget for these quarterly, or every three months. My quarterly budget is a little less because I need less. Similar to your weekly SLUSH Fund, once the money is used up, you are done, so spend wisely. If you don't use all the money in a quarter, you can roll that spending to the next quarter.

Financial fit budget example: Last year I used my entire Quarterly Ration budget to go to Japan and snowboard for a week. I rolled my ration forward every quarter and also used a little of my SLUSH fund so I could make that trip a reality. It only took me three quarters to fund a trip that I will remember for the rest of my life.

Traveling and Other Expenses

This is at the bottom of the budget for a reason. If all your money is used up from the previous budget categories, this bucket would go to zero. Personally, this is our favorite budget line, and we try to maximize this line each year. When you get to this point in your budgeting process, and it looks like you might not have enough money to travel, it's time to tone up your budget...along with your spending habits.

A financially fit person would never say *no* to travel; they would figure out where to cut unnecessary expenses in order to ensure a fun trip. The first line for us in this category is travel. Later in the book we will detail how to build a travel budget to maximize every trip you take. For now, look at what you spent the past couple years on travel expenses, or estimate what you think your trip(s) will cost, and put this in your budget around the date you believe you will travel.

After Travel comes "Other": Think about all the remaining leftover stuff that was not accomplished through the other buckets. Here are some examples of Other Expenses

- Birthday gifts
- Season ski passes
- Christmas gifts

Budget Tip: We budget $50 for each immediate family member's birthday presents, and we budget $500 total for Christmas gifts. Do we usually spend that much? No. We don't spend $50 dollars on everyone's gifts, and we don't spend $500 at Christmas. Instead, we think of creative ways to underspend in these categories so we can overspend in others. Most of the time we find cool crafts on Pinterest and make them for our family. We also never buy cards because they are ridiculously expensive for things that just get tossed immediately, we would much rather make them by pasting pictures of us with that friend or family member and writing a nice note. People love thoughtful gifts because it shows you spent time rather than just picking up something at the store

If you have not checked out our blog head over to thirtysomethingmillion-aire.com to see how we save on these items and more.

Step 7: The Final Rollup

At this point you will have your master budget spreadsheet. Great job! Hopefully, you learned some new skills along the way. You should now have a weekly budget for the entire upcoming year, or for the remaining part of the current year. How does your budget look? Do the numbers show you growing your cash or losing it? Your first pass at creating a budget might be forecasting you losing money every month. That is okay because this is the time to turn on your value detector and start searching for places to cut back. Reduce spending in areas that don't bring value to your life.

It's best to document what you need first, then focus on your wants and eliminate everything else. Get creative on reducing the needs so you can amplify the wants. Keep tweaking until you finalize the plan. While the process might be time intensive the first time, it will become easier with every update.

Updating Your Budget

The only way to successfully spend to your budget is to track your spending against your budget each week. When you are following your GPS to a location, the only way it knows how to direct you is because it knows exactly where you are at every given moment. A budget is the same; the only way to your long term goals is to track where you are every week.

Now that you have this new fancy tool, it's time to get busy use it. Building the budget is a small part of the transformation. The larger part of financial fitness is updating your progress. How can you celebrate a goal if you don't have the data to support the achievement of each milestone?

Every Monday morning, while you are drinking a cup of coffee out of your favorite mug, input spending from the prior week and see how you are tracking against your budget. The first few weekly updates may be more time consuming then you initially thought. But, as you form the habit of updating your spending each week, the process will speed up dramatically. After you master updating your budget, you will become an expert at understanding your spending habits. This new skill will create positive money habits that will enable you to eliminate wasteful spending. The savings you will realize from this weekly habit will not only transform your finances, it will help you channel money into what you truly value; your passions in life.

Updating your budget takes two simple steps:

First: calculate your net cash.

Net cash = total cash in your checking account *minus* total credit card balances (make sure to include any pending transactions). Many purchases take time to post to your account, but the money is already gone, so it is necessary to capture these items.

Second: input all your spending into the categories laid out in your budget.

Categorize each dollar you spent last week. If one category has been underspent, put those savings back into the budget at a later date. Or if you overspent, lower something in your budget for the upcoming weeks.

How do you know when you are done? We are projecting cash here, so after you have completed itemizing your expenses, you will come up with an ending Net Cash number for that week. That Net Cash number you are calculating must be equal to your actual Net Cash. Once they are equal, you are done. Nice work!

Budget Tip: Pay off your credit cards each week after your budget update is complete. When I say credit card balance, that is not a rolling a balance. Each week I have a credit card balance, because I buy everything on a credit card. After I get done updating all my spending, I pay off my balance. The habit of paying off your credit card balance each week will ensure that you never pay interest on a credit card. Also, paying each week keeps you from having a large bill at the end of the month.

I don't think of credit cards as debt; I view them as a convenient way to avoid carrying cash; plus I get a discount on everything I buy because I only use credit cards that offer great rewards like cash back or travel miles. Credit card companies lose money on financially fit people because they never pay interest to credit card companies, but they *do* take advantage of great credit card offers.

What to Remember

If you are not actively tracking something that takes you the most amount of time in your life to create (money), then your time is being wasted. If you overspend in part of your budget, but don't reduce spending in other categories, you will end up in the same position as you are today. Stick to it no matter what, this is the only way to find what you actually value in life.

As long as you track and stick to your budget, you can spend guilt free and live stress free because you know all your bases are covered, and you are on track to your goal.

How to Stick to a Budget and Enhance Your Life

Do you act differently when you are in church? At a football game? In front of family? In front of a new group of friends? Personal finance is driven by behavior.

> Groupthink (noun): a pattern of thought characterized by self-deception, forced manufacture of consent, and conformity to group values and ethics. (Merriam Webster)

An enemy to your budget is "groupthink." The larger the herd, the dumber the herd. Groupthink is very real and often causes a lapse in judgment. Have you ever been on a health kick and sat down at night and watch your significant other eating ice cream? I bet more than once, you have grabbed a spoon and dug into the chocolate chip cookie dough. Why does this happen? The deviation from your diet feels better if you eat the ice cream as a group. This lapse in your diet might not have happened if you were alone. The same can be said about a spouse or a friend spending money. If they are doing it, it's okay, right? Never fall victim to groupthink. You don't want to be average do you? If you make decisions that conform to the group, you will end up just that...average.

If groupthink is the enemy of good financial behavior, it is also the enemy of your budget. When you build your budget, you are in a quiet room without any distractions. In this environment you can build the perfect plan that makes sense for your life. The execution of staying on your budget is different. You are not in your controlled environment, you are with groups of people in situations that you cannot control. Don't let your environment dictate the results of your budget.

When you are in an uncontrolled environment, your behavior can become unpredictable. As you go through the first few passes of tracking your spending against your budget, you will most likely fail a couple times. Failure is normal, and failure is progress. If you stick to your overall budget, you will not have to reduce spending in areas of your life that you truly value. If you do *not* stick to your budget, however, you may have to redirect money from your travel fund because you had a really expensive night out with your friends. After this happens once or twice, you will say *No more* to overspending on the invaluable.

To assist with this and ensure you always stick to your plan, start making all your money decisions before you enter the spending situation. Make your mind up before you enter the uncontrollable environment. When you make the decision before you enter, you already know what your outcome will be and you will be happy when it's time to exit. Don't change for anything or anyone. You created your plan in a controlled environment, so make your decisions in the same environment. If you don't want something in the controlled environment, why would you all of a sudden want it in the uncontrolled environment? You don't. You are spending on impulse or due to external pressure. Don't let this behavior be the reason that keeps you from spending on what you actually want.

Have you ever had buyer's remorse? It's the worst. In the heat of the moment, you made a decision that, had you the time to think about, you would have acted differently. When this happens a feeling of remorse sets in. Impulsive decisions are the ultimate enemy to wealth. While impulsive spontaneous decisions are fun in the moment, they will ultimately leave you feeling down and asking, "Why did I do that?" If you ever want something in the heat of the moment, wait two days and see if you feel the same, rather than buying it on the spot. You will notice the things you think you cannot live without in that impulsive situation are things you actually don't really want or need. Take the time to clear your head. The worst time to make a financial decision is in a hurry.

CHAPTER 6

The Balance Sheet: Calculating Wealth

In order to improve, you need a benchmark for your current financial state. I consider the balance sheet a more "advanced" financial term/statement. The basics of it are easy, though, and this chapter covers how to build one for your financial world. Your balance sheet is, by far, the most important statement to understand. Once you start making decisions about how your spending and saving decisions affect your net worth, you will be much better off and start accumulating much more wealth. Let's get started with the basics.

Building Your Balance Sheet

As discussed earlier, your balance sheet is a snapshot of your net worth at any given time: *Assets you own minus the Liabilities you owe someone else (your debt)*. Net worth is the amount of money you would have in your bank account if you sold everything you owned and paid off all your debts. It's that simple.

This starts with your assets. An asset is something that holds value, like a $1 bill is 100 cents. Cash, cars, homes, and retirement accounts are examples of assets. The second part is your liabilities (debt). If you own a home and have a mortgage, then the bank has a lien on your property. That means that if you sold your home, you would have to pay off your loan in order for the bank to release the lien, so you have a liability to the bank. Credit card debt, auto and student loans are all examples of liabilities.

A balance sheet calculates the most important financial metric, your net worth. This is such an important measurement because it will help you understand how to make important financial decisions. I hardly ever think about how much cash I have in my bank account. For me, it's all about wealth. All too often, people are reluctant to put money into a 401(k), for example, because they don't get to see that balance in their checking account. But if you have a balance sheet, you will see how that money is increasing your net worth. If you are like me, you will also have this balance sheet forecasted out for over thirty years to track how much money you must save to hit a point where you could stop working...financial freedom. This, I like. It's what motivates me, and my balance sheet is the tool I use to gauge how we're doing financially.

Head over to thirtysomethingmillionaire.com to download a free template. After it's downloaded let's put some numbers into the template to calculate your net worth. An example of a balance sheet is contained in the picture below.

Personal Balance Sheet

Assets	Jan ----->	Dec
Checking Account	$	$
Stock Options	$	$
Car (Kelly Blue Book Value)	$	$
Home Value	$	$
Retirement Accounts	$	$
Other Investment Accounts	$	$
Total Assets	$	$
Liabilities		
Mortgage Balance	$	$
Auto Loan Balance	$	$
Credit Card Balance	$	$
Student Loan Balance	$	$
Total Liabilities	$	$
Personal Equity		
Net Worth (Assets minus Liabilities)	$	$

How do you build a balance sheet? Let dive in starting with assets.

Assets

Think about everything you own and determine its actual worth. The value of something is the amount you would receive if the item were to be sold. Obviously, cash and investments are easy because the account balance is how much the asset is worth. Things like cars and homes are a bit trickier. Never overestimate the value of something, or your balance sheet will be inaccurate. Remember sandbagging? For example, if the Kelley Blue Book values your car at $10,000, put it on the balance sheet for $9,000. Just like you are trying to hit budget goals, you will also be trying to hit net worth goals. Never let the sale of an item reduce your net worth by overvaluing them.

I always underestimate value of assets because when it comes time to sell, I am pumped up to get more than the estimated value on my balance sheet so I can inch closer to my net worth goal for the year.

Common Asset Categories on a Balance Sheet:

- Cash (savings and checking accounts)
- Investments (401(k), certificates of deposit, investment accounts, etc.)
- Cars: Kelly Blue Book can help estimate value.
- House: The market price for your house and any other investment property. Note that when determining the value of your home, factor in the real estate transaction costs you will incur when selling. Commissions can be up to 6% of the selling price of your home.
- Other assets: Gold in your basement, diamond ring, a piece of moon rock? Anything you own that you could sell if you absolutely needed to. Most things you buy have a limited life and you will never end up selling them. I have a small amount on my balance sheet for this line, which includes things like my wife's wedding ring, furniture, other nice jewelry, etc. Don't overstate this section because you will think you are wealthier than you really are.

Liabilities

Let's understand how much you owe your family, friends, the government, the banks, etc., so we can determine your net worth. Once you lay everything out, it may be shocking just how much you owe. As you go through each of your loans, document the interest rate. This will be important when we talk about attacking the debt. Your first step will be to identify the loan with the highest interest rate, and start prepaying the principal on that loan until it is 100% paid off, then on to the next one. More on this later.

Common Liability Categories on a Balance Sheet:

- Mortgage: How much do you owe on your house? Second house? Third house? You get the idea here. Log into your loan provider's website and find your outstanding balance and interest rate.
- Auto loan: If you have a car payment, figure out how much you owe on each car. Again, log into your loan provider's website to see the outstanding balance and interest rate.
- Student loans: Log into your loan provider's website to see the outstanding balances and associated interest rates.
- Credit card debt: How much do you owe? If you carry a balance, what is the interest rate?
- Other debt/liabilities: What other things have you financed? Furniture, rings, personal loans, home equity lines of credit, etc. you get the idea.

Net Worth

The sum of your total assets minus the sum of your total liabilities is your net worth. Pretty simple, right? If this is the first time you have ever looked at this metric, it may surprise you, but don't let it freak you out. If you are not where you want to be or thought you would be, then you are still one step ahead because knowledge is power, and in order to get better, you have to have a benchmark.

Personal Balance Sheet Forecasting

Seeing my money forecasted out over a long period of time is what keeps me pushing to win in every present second. I have a personal balance sheet that forecasts each year until I'm sixty, based on conservative growth rates. I know that by the time I'm forty, my future children's' college will be paid for, my retirement will be funded, my house will be paid for, and maybe I can splurge and buy a couple cars. Does that sound crazy? You don't need a lot of money to get there. Now that you know how a balance sheet works, take a stab at forecasting all your balance sheet items over the next thirty years.

Updating Your Balance Sheet and Setting Goals

Want to be a millionaire? Start forecasting your balance sheet to determine how and when you will hit millionaire status. The balance sheet is all we use to set our household financial goals. We operate within the bounds of our cash budget and update our balance sheet monthly.

Why is this so important to forecast into the future? To help you understand how much you need to have saved at different stages in your life to achieve a net worth later in life you can thrive on. This is easy now that you have all your investment accounts, assets, and liabilities in one place. You can forecast how your assets will grow and the timing of reducing your liabilities in the future. When forecasting how much money will grow in investments, use an 8% annual growth assumption. As we have discussed, 8% is the average historical return of the stock market, adjusted for inflation.

This number will be different for everyone. You can easily calculate this number by entering "retirement calculator" into a Google search. These calculators will walk you through a bunch of questions that you can answer with ease after building your budget and your personal balance sheet. After this is done, the calculator will pop out a number. The goal here is to figure out what the value of that number is today. Money grows, so if you need a certain amount at retirement and start saving early, you don't need to save that much because the money will grow over the years. For example, if you wanted to have $1 million dollars at age sixty, you only need around $100,000 dollars today if you have a thirty-year investment horizon. For example, I have calculated my "number" in retirement, so I figure out how much I need to save by a certain age to have that number when I'm sixty. Understanding what you need now is the important part.

Wealth, Not Cash

In the early stages of building wealth, most wealthy people are actually quite "cash poor," but what does that mean? Cash poor means you only keep the minimum amount of cash you need to get through the year (on top of your three to six months of safety net savings). Cash balances may grow as you save for large purchases, but it is always planned. Every other dollar made is funneled into increasing net worth. Any time there is extra cash, the extra cash is placed into investments that cannot be withdrawn, like paying down debt or investing in retirement accounts, etc. Wealthy people are in for the long game, and make sure every drop of cash is working as hard as possible.

When you are starting out in the adult world, you will be cash poor. Now that you know how a balance sheet works, let your net worth be your motivator, not how much cash you have in a bank account. The reason you are cash poor when you start out is that you have many one-time large purchases and a low starting income. Your first job doesn't pay a lot, and you need to buy a car, save for retirement, come up with a down payment on a house, buy furniture, etc. Think about all the large items you have to buy as you start out in life. All of these purchases should be one time in nature. The down payment savings for your house is a one-time occurrence, the furniture you buy is a one-time occurrence, and once you own your car, you will have equity in it, so you can trade it for the next one, etc. All these purchases are building blocks. Be patient. I know it might be hard not to have a lot of cash at this stage, but we know cash doesn't matter, net worth does. One day you will be done with these building-block expenses, and your income will increase. This is when the money starts to build up. It's a marathon not a sprint. Wealth is like an iceberg: you can see a little bit of it on the surface, but the bulk of its mass is hidden underwater.

Takeaways from the Balance Sheet

I know the previous section was a little dry and felt like a finance textbook, but it taught us that net worth is the primary goal. Now that you know how it works, think about how other people's balance sheets might look. Some folks may have a lot of really expensive assets like cars, homes, boats, and planes, but that doesn't necessarily mean they actually "own" them. They might have a large asset section on their balance sheet, but the liabilities section could be larger, which indicates a negative net worth. People who *look* like they are worth $1 million *are not* always worth $1 million.

Focus on *your* net worth. Make every decision thinking about the impact to your net worth. Having 1% down on a million-dollar house does not mean you're rich. Your BMW lease—which never even makes it onto the balance sheet because it's just a monthly cash payment (you don't ever own that car), does not mean you're rich. You are a millionaire when your assets are worth $1 million more than your liabilities. Don't get ahead of yourself by making yourself look rich; you are just stacking the cards against your future wealth.

CHAPTER 7

Eliminating Debt: The Debt Diet Plan

Everyone wants security in life, and your three to six months of safety net savings is just that. Before you can have a safety net, though, you do need to eliminate financial waste from your life. That financial waste is debt. If you do have debt and are ready to head down the elimination path, your first step is building a "mini safety net." Also known as your emergency fund.

Emergency Fund

Before paying down a dollar of debt, it's important that you get $1,000 to $2,000 in an emergency savings (this is your mini safety net). Do *not* incur any additional debt while building your emergency fund. Remember, we focus on net worth in this book, so if you rack up $1,500 in credit card debt to create a $1,500 emergency fund, then your net worth increased by $0. An emergency fund must be liquid cash in a savings account that is ready to use at any time without penalty for early withdrawal. The only activity this account should ever have is deposits. No bills, no direct debits, no credit card payments, nothing. Simply start putting the money in, saving however much you can and leaving it there until a true emergency forces you to use it, after which you begin to build it back up. You must have this emergency fund in place *before* paying down debt because it creates a small financial buffer, allowing you to accomplish your debt goals because you are covering any life events that could happen during the process.

How to Build Your Emergency Fund

"Keep only those things that speak to the heart, and discard items that no longer spark joy. Thank them for their service – then let them go."[15]

—Marie Kondo

I really want to emphasize here that it's best to try to build an emergency fund by selling things or hustling on the side. I do not want you to take money away from what should be used to pay down your debt. Get creative, and sell all the stuff you don't use or don't care about. Have a garage sale or sell online through websites like Craigslist, Poshmark, ThredUp, or eBay. If your financial position is precarious, it's probably because you bought too much stuff at some point. Along with kicking your habit for acquiring material things, sell the ones that no longer serve you. You are 100% committed, right? Your goal should be to sell enough items to put $500 to $1,000 in your emergency fund. Now you are rolling; you just knocked out two birds with one stone!

Selling your car can be another great place to kick-start your journey to financial fitness. If you already have a car that is relatively inexpensive, keep it. However, if you have financed an expensive car that is rapidly depreciating, think about selling it for something cheaper. If that monthly payment is what is holding you back from achieving your financial goals, it may be time to look at selling your car for a less expensive one.

After your emergency fund is stocked up, it's time to start putting those finances through their paces: trim the fat and get financially fit. I'm going to be honest; you will need to make some sacrifices in your life if you have a lot of debt. A little pain now for a lifetime of freedom is well worth it... don't let a mountain of debt intimidate you. Remember that removing a pebble from

---

[15] KonMari.com, accessed January 2019, https://konmari.com/pages/about.

the mountain each day with intention will turn that mountain into a molehill in no time.

Create Your Debt Diet Plan

When we talk about debt in this book, the only "good" debt is a mortgage, as long as you have not overextended yourself on your home purchase. The reason this is good debt to have is that mortgages typically have a low interest rate, and mortgage financing is a cheaper alternative to renting for the rest of your life. All other debt needs to go. Paying down your house is the pinnacle of financial freedom, but I don't think you need to aggressively attack this unless you want to. I believe a strategy of paying it down over fifteen years is a great plan. Now let's get to the other debt you might have.

The Higher the Interest Rate, the Larger the Drain on Your Net Worth

Time to start digging in on how to pay down debt. First, knowledge is power, and you need to know where you currently are because you know where you want to be in the future. You should have already documented this information, but if not, grab your computer and open a spreadsheet, or grab a notebook and a pen, or engrave these numbers on a tree outside. Whatever your method, document the following:

1. Get the balance of each loan you have.
2. Next to the balance, write the interest rate.

Take a step back and organize these debts by interest rate, ranking the debts by highest interest rate to the lowest. Why do I want you to organize your debt like this? Follow along with me. If you have a small loan at 4% and a larger loan at 17%, you want to pay the 17% loan down first because it will save you more in interest and have the greatest effect on your balance sheet. It's really pretty simple, and maybe this sounds like common sense, but I've found it's not clear to many people. You have the same amount of cash servicing debt each month, so you must allocate that money to what is going to give you the highest return and highest wealth impact.

Let's use those interest rates on a $100 example to clarify the concept. In a year, if you have a debt of $100 dollars with a 17% interest rate and another $100 debt with a 4% interest rate, what is the net worth impact of each rate annually? A 17% interest rate will cost you $17 over a year, and a 4% interest rate will cost you $4. Which one do you think you should pay off first? If you said 17%, you are correct. Clearly, that higher annual percentage rate has a greater negative net worth impact, and you want to eliminate those first.

That's it; there is nothing more to it. The formula is easy; it's the execution that is the tough part. Use every extra dollar you have to pay down your debts by largest interest rate first. Once you start to eliminate debt it will have a snowball effect. Each payment you knock out will leave you with extra cash that can be directed at your next debt and so on.

Eliminating Debt

When you start your debt-free journey, you will probably be excited. As you continue on your journey to becoming debt free, you could start to feel a bit down because you're putting all this money into debt reduction, but not getting anything to "show for this hard work." That is because you already own what you are paying for, and paying down debt is not a sexy way to spend money. You probably won't have your friends over to show them your balance sheet. You would prefer spending that money on an awesome TV so you can have your friends over and show them your cool purchase.

Paying down debt is purchasing your way to financial freedom, and once you get there, the nectar tastes so, so sweet. I want you to focus on the small wins throughout your debt-free journey. Celebrate each time you take chunks out of your debt. You are crushing it! It also helps to create milestones... whatever it takes to stay motivated.

Throughout this book, I will talk about different things you can do to save money. Things that you can cut out that really add no value in your life anyway, and you can shift those dollars into paying down debt. Since you don't truly care about those things in the first place, you will not notice their absence and can allocate those funds to paying down debt. The best feeling in life is being in control of your money and not letting it control you. Once you have eliminated debt and have safety walls surrounding your financial fortress, you *are* in control. Build in a reward for each time you knock out a debt to keep you motivated.

Acquiring Debt—Change Your Mindset

Let me ask you this question: If to avoid getting a loan on a product, you would only have to give up not having it for a short amount of time, would you do it? What if by doing so, you would never have to take out a loan again? Let's take cars as an example. If you finance your first car, odds are that when it comes time to get your next car, your current car will not be paid off, and you will need to finance the next one as well. You have now created a habit and are stuck in what we like to call "monthly payment syndrome." You will continue financing your cars and never give yourself enough time to pay off one to save for the next. All you are doing is living three years in the past.

What if rather than impulsively financing that car, you saved for two to four years to pay cash for it and by doing so you saved all that unnecessary interest, extra insurance, and financing fees, etc.? Once you buy the car, act as if you have a car payment and put that money into a savings account for the next car. You are already used to saving it, so just keep it going. Since you have planned and saved for this purchase, you will have enough money for the next car, and the car after that and the car after that. It's so much cheaper to "make" a car payment to yourself first, and continue to do so. Instead of paying for something after the fact, you are just paying for it at the actual time of purchase. This is living in the present versus financing something and living in the past. I know I have said this already but want to emphasize this point. You will only have to save up for something ONCE! It only takes waiting *one* time for a lifetime of owning. This goes for just about everything, it just takes that one time to wait and pay cash. Furniture? Save up. Credit card purchase? Save before swiping. By using this strategy, you will stay out of debt for the rest of your life. If you are going to pay monthly, you might as well pay yourself.

Ways to Limit Your Interest Expense in Your Debt Diet Plan

If, and only if, you are 100% committed to your debt diet plan, then check out these options for saving a little more money on your road to financial freedom. Let me throw a large disclaimer out here: Do not, and I repeat *do not*, open any of these products I'm about to discuss unless you are 100% committed to doing your reps to becoming financially fit and eliminating debt. Most personal finance books you read don't expose these products, and, in my opinion, are a little out of touch with today's society. In my opinion, if you open one of these products and pay off all the debt, calculate what you saved by moving the balance over and go spend *that* money (if and when you have the cash) on something as a reward. Because if you are going to pay off the debt anyway and figure out a way to do it that saves you a couple extra bucks, I think you deserve to treat yo-self.

1. Do you have equity in your house? One great way to consolidate high-interest consumer debt is with a home equity line of credit (HELOC). Say you have $20,000 in high-interest credit card debt. Instead of paying 16% interest, which could cost you almost $3,200 over the course of a year, which in turn makes it even harder to pay off due to this extra expense, you could consolidate your credit card debt and transfer it to a HELOC. Depending on your credit, a HELOC will carry a significantly lower interest rate. The interest rate is lower than a credit card rate because the debt is secured by the equity in your house.

In this example let's assume you can open a home equity line of credit for $20,000 at a 5% interest rate. Great, open it, and the next day pay off your entire credit card balance. By doing this, you just shifted $20,000 worth of debt from a 16% interest rate to a 5% interest rate. Get your calculator out.

How much does that save you during a year? The answer is a savings of almost $2,200 a year. Wow, would I rather spend $2,200 on interest expense or have a $2,200 increase in my net worth? The answer to that question should be obvious. Now, get focused on paying this off... then boom: balance paid off, no credit card debt. Consolidating your debt and making yourself the bank just saved a boat load in interest expense. I want to make this clear, once you have debt consolidated to a HELOC, you have to make it a priority to pay it off as fast as you can. If don't pay this off quickly, you are not saving yourself any money.

2. No home to pull equity from? Look into credit cards that offer a free balance transfer and 0% annual percentage rate (APR) for an introductory period. This is a no-brainer, but *only* make this move if you do your due diligence and find a card that has both a $0 charge to transfer the balance and a 0% APR introductory offer. These introductory zero-percent offers typically range from eight to sixteen months. In order for this to make sense, it needs to cost you nothing, zero, zilch. If you are passionate about paying off your credit cards for good and never accumulating credit card debt again, these balance transfer cards are amazing. You can then multiply the power of every dollar you are using to pay down your debt, because you no longer have to pay for interest expense.

Let me throw in another disclaimer. You *must* be financially fit when opening a 0% interest card to make sure you never miss a payment. Most of these cards are like navigating a fee minefield. If you ever miss a payment, your 0% introductory offer disappears, and you'll be charged whatever high interest rate comes with the card. The minute you open the card, set up an automatic payment for $7.00 more than your first month's required payment and have it automatically paid seven days before your payment is actually due. Leave the card at home and never spend a dollar it. After that just let it go on autopilot. When you scrape up even more money, make larger payments, but always leave the automatic payment you set up for $7.00 more than the first monthly payment seven days before it's due. This ensures that you will never miss a payment or pay too little on a payment by mistake. You should actively track this each month to make sure the payment processed. Boom, by using this strategy you just saved a large amount of interest expense.

Getting out of debt is decidedly unglamorous. But tracking your progress on your balance sheet and watching your net worth increase during your debt-reduction journey makes it oh so glorious.

Breaking the Chain of Debt

The real problem with debt in the long run is that you are conditioning yourself only to consider the monthly payments, and end up paying loads of interest expense, fees, etc. I have said this a lot and I will say it again...if you cannot afford to buy something with cash, *you cannot afford it*. Don't take this the wrong way, instead, take it as an opportunity or a challenge to make it happen. Do you really want it? How hard are you willing to work to get it? Anyone can go out and finance something. If you brag that you bought an item and think you are cool after financing it, the reality is the bank owns it, not you. It really sucks having to pay for something you already have in your possession.

I have been in this situation before and it was a great learning experience for me. After I graduated from college, I was driving around in an old Toyota Camry. I just landed my first real job where I was making a lot more money than before, and I felt really rich. Because I was so "rich," I decided I deserved a badass, lifted, four-door Jeep Wrangler. Without doing much research, I hopped on down to the dealer to pick out my new toy. Yes, it was used, I wasn't the most informed at that age, but still knew not to buy new cars. Since I didn't have enough cash to pay for it, I walked out of the dealer financing 50% of that Jeep.

That first month I felt amazing, *how cool am I*? I could afford the monthly payment, and I didn't think I would mind it that much. I was severely wrong. I hated myself for having that loan. The interest I paid irritated me because I knew it was a waste of money, but what really infuriated me was the fact that I had to continue to pay for something I already had. It was tough to make myself pre-pay on that loan, because I already had the car in my possession, but I put my head down and got busy. Flash forward eight months and the car was paid off. Flash-forward another four months, and I bought a house. The ambition I got from having a car payment was huge. I cut every expense to the bare minimum, I hustled to make extra cash on the side (I probably went to extremes; you are probably not surprised). I have never had a car payment again, and I never will.

Moral of the story? Saving for something is fun because you get to look forward to getting it. It's like planning a vacation. You set a date and cross off your calendar each day until that day arrives. Waiting for something like that is as therapeutic as going on vacation in my opinion. After grinding at your job day in and day out, having something to look forward to will fuel your fire. Instead of punishing your future self with debt, establish a laser focus to achieve what you want now. You have to pay for it anyway, why waste money paying more for it due to financing fees and interest? You will end up a better person from the experience of saving for something like this. Who knows, maybe you will do something to make some extra cash and make a career out of it. At the end of the day, and trust me on this one, the accomplishment you will feel when you have the ability to pay cash will make you love whatever it is you are buying a lot more.

CHAPTER 8

Understanding the Total Cost

This one is huge: financially fit people wrap their minds around the entire cost of something. Cars are a great example. Many consumers have no clue how much wealth a car costs them each year (think insurance, gas, maintenance, depreciation, tires, registration, taxes, the whole lot). The all-in cost is not just the sticker price of the car, it is much, much more. Before you buy anything take a step back and determine all the numbers. What is the true total cost? A great site to research the five year cost of ownership for a car is Edmonds.com. Log in and research a car you're interested in. I guarantee you the total cost of ownership will blow your mind.

Another example are pets. Let's say you want to get a dog. Not a problem—you can adopt a dog for very little money up front, but there are many other costs associated with dog ownership. The second you take that adorable little puppy home; you need to give him his scheduled shots as he approaches a year old. You also have annual check-ups, and medications (i.e., heartworm or flea and tick prevention). This assumes your dog is healthy and never needs any other medication or surgery. You will have to buy dog food, toys, collars, leashes, and probably a dog crate. You have to groom them and get their teeth cleaned. Say you want to go on vacation? You have to either board your dog or get a friend to watch them. They can destroy your house, kill your grass, make your car dirty, etc.

Sounds like I really hate dogs, but it's actually the opposite. I love my two dogs so much, and I will always have dogs. I'm just very aware of what everything costs, and the cost is worth it to me due to the value my dogs bring to my life. The problem, especially with dogs, is that people tend to only think about the initial cost to buy the dog. Remember this before you buy anything, think about how much it will cost you each *year in total*. If you are okay with that number, proceed. I think about the total cost with everything I buy; shocker, I know. When it comes to money, I don't like surprises.

Knowledge Makes Money Predictable.

Another way to think about the total cost of something is to remember what it took to acquire that money you are about to spend. Some purchases are well worth the sacrifice, some are not worth it at all. A good example of this is thinking about the physical activity needed to burn off a treat that you love to eat. Did you know that a cup of Ben and Jerry's Ice cream has around 540 calories? In order to burn 540 calories you would need to run around four or five miles, do an hour on the Stairmaster, or complete circuit training for almost an hour to get those calories burned off your body. If you thought of this every time you put that spoon to your mouth, I guarantee you would start to think differently about how much you consume.

The same goes for money. When you are getting ready to spend a large chunk of cash, think about what it took to earn that money. How many hours, weeks, days, months or years?

How much do you save every year? Take your total savings for the year and divide it by 2,088, which is the total amount of business working hours in a year. This calculates how much savings you earn per each hour of work. Now let's do some math. Take the total price of the item you are looking to purchase and divide by your hourly saving rate that we just calculated. That equation will give you the total number of hours you worked to save enough money for what you are about to buy.

Say you *save* around $20,000 each year and you want to buy a new TV that costs $1,500. How many hours will it take you to earn enough money for this purchase? You would have to put in 156 hours, or over nineteen working days, for that TV. Is the time sacrifice of nineteen days of work worth it? Maybe it is, but maybe it isn't. That is up to you to decide. A TV might be worth it, but let's calculate the hours worked for the purchase of a $30,000 car. In this same example, a $30,000 car would take you 1.5 *years* of work or over 3,100 hours. I know it hurts to think about things like this, but hey, this is reality.

Now let's think about that new car in retirement dollars. If you are spending $30,000 that means you are not saving $30,000. If you saved that $30,000 and let that amount compound 30 years at an 8% interest rate, you could have around $300,000.

These examples highlight the total cost of what you are purchasing. Every purchase is a sacrifice; understand the total cost to decide which ones are worth it. It's important that every purchase adds value in your life because it's costing you a lot more time and future savings than you might think.

Hidden Fees

"*Please read the fine print for a list of all our fees." This stuff drives me nuts. Understand the entire cost before you ever sign up for something. One industry that really does well on hidden fees is wealth management (for example, financial advisors). You give them money to invest, but you never have to pay them anything. What a deal. However, if you read your statements closely, you will find an array of management, transaction, balancing, and other fees hidden in the cost of doing business with them. I don't expect anyone to do something for free, but it is important to understand what the services actually cost. Work with reputable companies who will clearly lay out the fine print.

Mortgage companies are notorious for charging fees that are both hard to find and understand. One large misconception is that taking out a mortgage or refinancing one is free. No service in life is free. Why would people think like this? Because they don't have to pay with money up front. These fees are wrapped into your loan whether you realize it or not. They usually appear via an increased total loan amount or a slightly higher interest rate. When you get a mortgage have the broker clearly lay out the fees and explain exactly what they are charging you for. Don't let them get away with telling you, "It's only one-half of a percentage point." That one-half percentage point over thirty years will cost you a significant amount of money.

Many industries will wrap costs into their products, and that is okay as long as you are aware of the total cost before you make a purchase.

The Up Sell

One thing I would like to talk about in understanding the total cost is the "up sell." A good example of this is Spirit Airlines. Because Spirit's advertised airfares are generally lower than other airlines, people often think they are getting a great deal. However, given all the incidental costs incurred when you fly with them, the final cost tends to be the same as a full-service airline, yet the service and experience is worse.

Many consumers are conditioned to follow through on a sale once we have put out some effort. The more pages we click through, the more we remember that advertised initial offer on page one. The issue here is that once we click "complete transaction" on page five, we are spending vastly more than we originally thought. Shopping around for a good deal is always a solid choice, but don't shop based on the first page or the advertised price; you need to compare apples to apples if you want to make a decision about which airline to fly. Companies like Frontier and Sprint will seem cheaper than, say, Southwest at first glance, but the difference between those companies is that Southwest is upfront and gets right to the final price, which includes baggage fees and everything else, and the other airlines don't. Be a savvy shopper and compare the *final* price. You will find the prices are not going to be materially different from one another, and you will get a better flying experience from those other airlines.

Paying Up Front

If a company requires you to pay monthly, obviously you have no choice. If they do offer options to pay annually or semiannually, do it because you will often get a discount. A great example is car insurance. I know paying for your auto insurance in full for a six-month duration seems like a lot of money. Go ahead and slap yourself on the noggin, because many times you can actually save money over the six-month period if you pay up front versus monthly. Yes, that first month you have to come up with more money. After that six months is over, you have saved money. Cha-ching! You are going to have to pay for it anyway; wouldn't you rather pay less?

Direct Debits

A direct debit is authorizing a company to debit money out of your bank account on a recurring basis based on an agreement you signed for convenience (often for subscriptions like HBO, Dollar Shave Club, FabFitFun, etc). Take control of your money and keep these direct debits to a minimum. If you do authorize a direct debit, you must track these debits each month. This way you can figure out if the product you are buying is actually worth your time and money. Ten dollars here and there goes unnoticed by the average person, and by the end of the year, you may have spent a couple of grand and had no clue the money was removed from your account.

I once worked in the treasury department for a large corporation. This company generated over $500 million in annual revenue. Do you think they allowed vendors to direct debit the accounts? Never. Every invoice went through an approval process. The amount of the invoice dictated the appropriate level of approval. People with higher titles (like a vice president) could authorize approval on higher dollar amounts. Companies don't allow vendors the opportunity to directly debit their account, so why should you?

Certain things are okay to be direct debited out of your account: utilities, cell phone payments, rent, mortgage, savings withdrawals, and things of this nature. These bills are something that you have no control over and are necessities in life. You still need to keep an eye on these expenses each time they remove money to ensure they don't add an extra zero or change your billing rate, etc. You should limit direct debits on anything that is not a recurring need that you cannot live without, and be sure to actively keep track of these withdrawals.

Why do companies want to set you up on automatic withdrawal? Because they don't need your approval each time they take money from you. Once they have all your information set up, it's hard to cancel it, and companies know this, which is why they make you jump through hoops to cancel. They know you won't cancel your subscription because you forget about it each month until they bill you. Then you say you will cancel next month before it hits again, and you forget. They entice you with convenience and keep you imprisoned by an inconvenient process to cancel. They also know you might not want to buy the product next month or next year, so they want to make that decision for you. As we talked about, some of these are so small that you may not even notice it. Take control of your money.

Think Like a Millionaire

Here's some advice to live by: **If you cannot pay for it in cash, you cannot afford it.**

Save cash to pay for assets up front. If you cannot afford it, wait until you can. Remember when I said earlier that wealthy people start cash poor? That is because they are not financing anything, they wait until they have the cash to buy everything. Here is a common money myth debunked. When purchasing something, for example a car, I often hear people say they don't want to dump all their cash into the car; they want to keep it in a checking account, so they finance the car instead. I believe you probably don't really want that car enough then. Don't fall into the trap of thinking that just because the money is not in your bank account after the purchase that it is gone.

Learn to Buy Everything with Cash

Remember your balance sheet? Assets include the value of a car. Even if it makes the wealthy person feel cash poor at the moment, they will buy it with cash, because doing so saves them so much over the long term. This also helps them understand the total cost of the car. A monthly payment hides what the car is actually costing you. Let's explore this a bit further. What does a car purchase look like buying cash vs. financing? Buying with cash up front is so much cheaper than financing over the long term. Yes, $200 a month seems cheaper than $10,000 up front, but in the long run, you will pay much more for that car in the form of interest and other fees the bank will charge to use their money. Let's break down this example.

You may say, "I don't want to wrap up all my cash in a car, so I will use financing. It's only $200 a month, and I will still have that $10,000 in the bank." How about we take a look at your balance sheet? If you take a loan out to buy a $10,000 car, you have $10,000 in the assets column, *and* $10,000 in the Liabilities column. If you buy a car with cash, your cash line goes down $10,000, but your assets column goes up $10,000 (as of the day of the purchase; assets like cars will depreciate over the long term, but I'm isolating that variable).

	Buying Cash	**Financing**
Cash	(10,000)	-
Closing Costs for loan	-	(500)
Other Financing charges	-	(500)
Car	10,000	10,000
Total Assets	-	9,000
Car Loan	-	10,000
5 Yrs of interest	-	1,300
Total Liabilities	-	11,300
Net Worth	-	(2,300)

Interest is a huge factor on the debt side and it greatly increases the cost of anything that is financed. Most people turn a blind eye to interest expenses and only focus on the payment, but that is a myopic and costly mistake. When financing a car, you also have to pay closing costs to the bank supplying the financing and also the interest on the debt for the duration of your loan. Many times when you finance, you can be required to purchase a warranty and insurance policies like GAP insurance. At the end of the day, you've just spent thousands more by getting a loan just because you didn't want to "spend" the cash. Instead of getting a deal, you increased the price of what you bought by 10% to 20%.

Think about wealth, not cash. You need to approach every decision with the wealth effect of each transaction in mind. It's hard to save and it might hurt seeing money leave your checking account but you must save up before you buy anything. Remember, if you don't have the cash to buy something, just wait until you save enough to cover the cost. When you finance something, you are just paying more for it unnecessarily which increases the total cost.

CHAPTER 9

Identifying Value

We have talked a lot about only spending money on things that bring value to your life, but how do you identify those things? We are finally to that point. The best way for me to understand value is an exercise of reliving my favorite moments in each day, last week, month, year, and in my whole life. I'm going to present a few strategies for you, so grab a piece of paper and a pen or create a document on your computer to lay out your ideas. Apart from the lists we are about to create, make sure to keep notes on your phone in case something pops into your mind at a later date. Actively thinking about this and journaling your thoughts will help uncover what is valuable to you. Let's get started.

We know that earning money is difficult, so it's important that you only spend money on things that enrich your life, so that you can live the life you love. Before you can live the life you love, you need to figure out *what* you love.

Your Lists

First I will help you understand what you want, then we will figure out what you don't want. Having a laser-focus on what you want *and* on eliminating useless expenses will have a massive positive impact. This behavior will lead to saving money from the useless things and funnel that money into the life impacting ones. You can save money and still do what you love; in fact, you can accomplish both.

What You Love

Listing the things you enjoy is probably not what you expected from a personal finance book, but it's important to do what you enjoy while saving money to stay motivated.

However, you have to be realistic for this exercise to work. It is best to focus on things you have already done because you know how those experiences made you feel. For example, I have no clue how owning the most expensive Ferrari would feel, so writing that down is pointless and unrealistic. Everyone has different experiences, activities, or routines they enjoy.

A useful practice is to relive events in your mind. Since we all know that it's hard for humans to relate to an unknown future, we need to focus on the past. What is it that really drives you? What in the past have you looked forward to that made you happy? Reminisce about the happiest times in your life.

Start by writing your favorite thing you did this month. Was it attending a yoga class with your friends? Running a marathon? Or going to that new movie you were dying to see? Next, think about the best moments you have had in the last year. Trip to Europe? Spending a week with your family? Or building a treehouse in your backyard? Hopefully, from this exercise, you can surprise yourself with some activities you love that you have not done in a while.

If you're having a hard time recalling value add events, put a reminder in your phone every day at 9:00 a.m. Have the reminder ask the question, "What did you do yesterday that made you happy?"

What Would You...?

Now it's time to play a game called, "What would you...?" If you are having trouble thinking about what you love or value, answer the questions below to help you recognize what you value in life.

- I would eat dinner at home all week to make sure I had enough money for _____.
- What would you love to read a book about?
- What would you love to write a book about?
- What would you do for free?
- What did you love to do as a child?
- What would your friends say you are most passionate about?
- If you had all the money in the world, what would you choose to fill your day with?
- What are your favorite weekend activities?
- What are your favorite hobbies?
- What was your favorite part of last week?
- What was your favorite part of last month?
- What was your best memory from last year?

You will most likely start to see a common theme in the answers to these questions. Highlight them and note them as the life categories in which you see value.

What Wouldn't You?

Now turn the tables, and figure out what you are currently spending money on that isn't important to you. The best way to accomplish this is to grab your credit card statement and a highlighter. Let's see where you actually spent your money. Highlight all the expenses that fall into the following categories:

- I don't remember it.
- I couldn't care less about it.
- It was a waste of money.
- It was too expensive.

This is your list of the things you can cut out of your budget, which will cut them out of your life. If you don't need it, don't want it, and cannot remember it, then why spend money on it? If you don't remember purchasing it, then it wasn't a value add. I want you to eliminate spending that does not fuel your passions so you can channel that money into items and experiences that do. If the money spent didn't add value, you will not notice cutting it out, but you will notice your increasing disposable income.

Lastly, when going through your credit card statement put a star with a different colored pen/pencil next to things you loved or items that sparked a memory of joy. These items should correlate with your "wants" list we created earlier. If you found some new items you loved, add them to the "wants."

From these exercises, you should have two lists. Finding out what you *don't* love is just as impactful as figuring out what you *do* love. By classifying your expenditures in this way, you will be able to save money and direct it toward the things you actually value. I like to call this "Having your cake and eating it too."

Amplify Savings and Fun

Now that you have an idea of what you don't value, let's determine how to eliminate that financial waste out of your life. I have outlined some ways I removed the non-value from my life and allocated those savings to fuel my passions. Since the spending never added value to my life, I'm not giving up anything by removing it from my life. Now remember that what I value and what you value are different, so you may think some of these examples are a little extreme. But you will most likely be amused too. The point here is to save money on the "non-value" expenditure and allocate it to your value-add expenditures.

1. Spending money to eat out during the work week does not add value to my life. I consider using my lunch hour to leave the office in search of food a waste of both time and money. Since time is precious, I prefer to use my lunch hour to complete my workout

for the day. Working out during lunch keeps me from having to do it after work, which means I get home faster. I value spending time with my wife, hanging out with friends, and enjoying my hobbies after work. In order to make all of this possible, my wife and I plan and meal prep each of our lunches for the week. I estimate you can save between $100 and $200 each month or almost $2,000 a year by just packing your lunch. And because my lunch is already prepped, I can eat it while I work, which gives me the time to work out. This is a total win-win for me.

2. Spending money on alcohol at restaurants or sporting events...I will pregame before I enter an event. When I go out to eat, I'm going out for the food and the atmosphere. A beer is a beer to me. Although I do like to have one with my meal, I will never order more than one at a restaurant. I would rather spend my money on 1,000 other things before I pay the 1,000% mark-up on alcohol. Therefore, I will keep pre-gaming.

3. Paying for a haircut...I mean how hard can it be? I absolutely hate spending money on haircuts, and I think it's a pretty simple process. Instead of spending $20 to $40 at the barber every month, I spent $18 on Amazon for a Wahl hair clipper kit when it went on sale. My wife is now my barber. I still budget for this expense every month, but since I'm creative in how I approach it, I never spend money on this category. I usually spend my savings from this category on concert tickets or going out to dinner with friends.

4. Roses are red, bees make honey, greeting cards are a waste of money. Paying upwards of $6 for a card is a giant waste of money. Instead of buying that $6 dollar card, make one for free. I do this every year, for every occasion, and the recipients always light up when they receive them. Yes, you save money, but you are also showing your special someone how much you care because you put in the time and effort into making a custom card. Anyone can buy a card; show them you care by making one. Here is what you do...

- Gather Pictures: snag three to eight photos of you and that special someone. Grab pictures from highlights during your year.
- Paste those pictures into PowerPoint and make a collage. Paste the pictures so they fit on only half of the slide (you need to have 50% of the slide blank so you can fold the card).
- Print off the slide and fold it in half. Inside of the card write a heartfelt message.
- Your recipient will melt when they see that you went the extra mile to create a custom card with a custom message, and they get to see the pictures of you two together on the front.

4. Need Furniture? New furniture is expensive and is often not made in a quality manner. Ikea particle boards and cheap hardware? No thank you. Instead, buy used furniture and refurbish it to look the way you want. Older furniture is often made of solid wood and will last far longer than the cheap stuff out there today. Plus, you will get a massive discount because new furniture is worth a fraction of what you paid the day you bring it home. Another great option is purchasing high quality pieces from a consignment store. These stores carry high quality, lightly used, furniture at a steep discount.

5. Buying gas with your groceries: Does your grocery store offer fuel points with each purchase at the store? If so, you will most certainly have fuel points to turn into savings when you locate the gas pump at your regular grocery store. While these gas stations may not always be in the most convenient locations, it's always worth a slight detour. As I have said, I relate most things to the price of Chipotle. Maybe I forgot my lunch one day, so how do I make up for it? Usually, we rack up around $0.40 to $0.60 per gallon in credits each month. I have a thirty-six-gallon fuel tank in my truck, and if I wait until my fuel tank is nice and low, I can

save upwards of $18 per fill-up. That is easily two Chipotles, so I could go out to lunch twice if I wanted to.

CHAPTER 10

Maximizing Every Dollar

When thinking about what you want to buy, also think about what you would get for it if you needed to sell the item. One thing I have learned is that most products have a limited useful life, then people change their minds and sell them or give them away.

Nine Products with the Worst Resale Value

The following is a list of products to think twice about before you purchase them new. Also take a look at the used market to buy these products and save yourself boat loads of money. Speaking about buying used, I think it's a lot more fun. It feels like a game of strategy, and I like to win. Plus the better the deal I get on a quality product the more I will enjoy that product.

1. Cars - we already know how quickly they depreciate. Buy used and let someone else pay for the depreciation.

2. Computers and personal electronics - When the new product hits the shelves, buy the prior year model. You will get a steep discount. If you chase the newest model, you will pay a large markup.

3. Home decor - Just like furniture, home decorations are worth almost nothing after you buy them. Let someone else spend the

money and get a deal on it used. Purchase holiday decor after the holidays when they are deeply discounted to use the following years.

4. Furniture - People are always swapping out their furniture; you can typically pick up very high-end items for 50% to 70% off the original prices. Another option is refurbishing older, well-built pieces.

5. Hunting and outdoors equipment - Find someone who was hoping to get into a sport and decided, "This isn't for me." They will end up selling brand-new, top-of-the-line gear for cheap.

6. Jewelry - this is a fast depreciator and overpriced to begin with; buy it used and save a bunch.

7. Mountain or road bikes - I have always purchased used bikes, and you can typically get 50% off on a two-to three-year-old bike. People usually buy them, never use them, and then sell them.

8. Time-shares - Don't even get me started; they are horrible places to put your money, and they are not investments. Just pay for your travel when you travel.

9. Video games - wait until a video game is a few months old and buy it used from stores such as GameStop.

Making Extra Money

Once your budget is built and you are sticking to your weekly goals, it is human nature to want more things. How can you get those extra things without breaking your budget?

Everyone loves extra money for an unlimited number of reasons. There are many different ways to make money that can be devoted to off-budget spending. I love side hustles because they are freedom multipliers. Whether you want to attack debt faster or buy that special item that was not in your budget. The deal my wife and I have is any money we make on the side we get to spend on anything we like. If you put in the extra work, you should reap the reward. We call this "off-budget spending cash."

Side hustles also help give your SLUSH Fund spending a break. And who knows, maybe your side hustle turns into something that becomes your full time passion job. Either way, use the "what you love" list as your motivation, and use the examples below as your execution for obtaining extra money.

Ten Ways to Earn Extra Money

1. Sell Your Stuff

One person's trash is another person's treasure. My motto is that if I have not used it within the last year, I will either donate (if I cannot sell if for over $15), or sell the item. During the last month I made $300 just by selling old things that were lying around the house. If you don't use it, sell it. I always have something for sale because I like to give my budget a break.

2. Dog Walking

We live in a crazy time in which you can make money walking people's dogs. Check out wag.com, the Uber of dog walking. What a way to make extra money. This really is knocking two birds out with one stone. If I ever see a dog out and about, I always have to run up and say hello and pet them. The positive energy that dogs give off just makes your day better. Why not skip the gym membership (saving money) and get your exercise while walking a furry friend?

3. Dog Sitting

Keeping with the dog theme, check out rover.com, the Airbnb for dogs. Hang out with the best animals on the planet in the comfort of your home. Not traveling for Christmas? This is a great time to make some extra cash because you can charge much higher rates due to demand, since everyone is traveling and needs a dog sitter. Do this around the holidays to pay for all your holiday shopping.

4. House Sitting

I love house sitting. If you can find a few people who trust you, you can be their go-to solution for when they travel; it's an easy way to make extra money. We love to house sit and feel like it's a mini vacation because we are staying somewhere new. Take a mini vacation and get paid for it.

5. Referee for a Sport You Love

You can ref hockey, baseball, lacrosse, basketball... really any sport. A lot of the time the games will be local and close to home. Not to mention you can write off the gear, food you eat, and the mileage it takes to get to the games. Sometimes, they will have tournaments in cool places like Vail, Colorado. A friend of mine who refs hockey games will get invited to ref out-of-town games. They pay your lodging for the weekend, and offer a per-diem to cover all your food that weekend. Get the per-diem and eat on the cheap for even a larger money boost.

6. Airbnb Host

As someone who manages their own Airbnb, I can tell you from experience, it is a lot of work. It's not the most challenging work, but you have to dedicate time each week. Many people running Airbnbs will pay to outsource the work. You can take over the hosting duties for one or multiple Airbnbs and make great money preforming these tasks. You can automate most of the duties, reducing your time spent while making the same amount of money. If you are interested in hosting, head over to thirtysomethingmillionaire.com to find Airbnb best practices from a super host.

7. Uber or Lyft Driver

This is a no-brainer; if you have a car that gets good gas mileage, driving occasionally for Uber or Lyft is a great way to earn extra money. It isn't necessary to take up all your time driving. Just turn your car into an Uber when you are done with work and take someone home on your way home. Easy money, and you are not taking much time out of your day.

8. Crafting

Visit etsy.com to see all of the crafts people are selling. Consumers are drifting away from the huge department stores because they want different and unique items, and Etsy is a great place to buy them. Come up with an idea like a state flag painted on reclaimed wood, or build picture frames out of old fence posts. I'm not the most creative person, but, trust me, if you think something is cool or looks cool, millions of other people will want it too. You can get the supplies cheaply and spend a weekend mass-producing a product. After that, post it and start fulfilling orders.

9. Part-Time Waiter or Bartender

Waiters and bartenders make more money than you'd think. And it's a social thing too. Pick up shifts after work or on the weekends. These jobs can generate a lot of cash if you are good at them.

10. Blogging

Write weekly about passions or frustrations or both. You will be amazed that you can make money from website traffic and advertising. And even if you don't make any money, you will be surprised at how many free things you can get from doing this. Many people who have blogs get tons of free merchandise shipped to them and get to attend events for free. Simply take a couple pictures at the event and write about it later. Instagram is a good avenue for this. Easy peasy, and you get to experience events for free. Maybe not $1,000 in cash, but hey, you would have probably spent money doing a different activity, so you are saving money by getting to go to events for free.

CHAPTER 11

Focus on Needs until You Can Afford What You Want

There is a big difference between someone who is cheap and someone who is value oriented. I don't like to spend money, but when I do, I'm going to buy a quality product. Or said another way: I will never purchase a lower-priced item if the quality of the product is poor. I will either not buy it or buy the best one I can afford. Sure I end up spending a little more at first, but I save over the long-term because cheap items have to be replaced more frequently.

Quality Saves Money in the Long Run

Let's take dress shoes for example. Fake leather shoes are usually one third the price of high-end, real leather shoes, although, on the rack, they look very similar. They will look similar until the first day you wear them, then they will quickly fall apart and look like cheap, fake leather shoes. Good leather shoes can last three times as long as fake leather shoes. If you need something, it's much better to invest in a quality product or refrain from buying anything at all. Over the long term, you will spend much more money and time buying the cheap items over and over again. Just spend the money up front on a quality product, and you will not have to replace it as often. You get what you pay for, and I don't know about you, but I would rather not set foot into a mall more than I have to.

This thought process goes for anything really. People are often tricked by the initial outlay of money, but they lose sight of how many times they'll actually have to replace something. On the day of the purchase, people have a tendency to think less money spent is savings earned. This behavior is then repeated as you walk back into the same store to purchase the same thing sooner than you would have if you bought the quality product first.

Tires for your car are another great example. They are all the same right? They are round pieces of rubber. No, cheap tires have less durability, poor handling quality, less stopping power, and perform worse in the rain and snow. The main factor here is durability. Not only are you more prone to getting a flat tire, which will lead you to replace them anyway, but the tread on these tires will deteriorate much faster. Next time you are looking to buy tires focus on the mileage rating. This will tell you how many miles this tire should last. On cheaper tires, you will notice they are rated to last half as long as quality tires, but they are only 25% cheaper. If you think about it, 50% of tire life for a 25% discount is a terrible deal. The cheap tires will get you back into the tire shop sooner, which will have you reaching into your wallet faster. Buy the quality product the first time around.

One last example. I love buying Lululemon work pants. Lululemon makes men's work pants? Yes. They are, however, $130—expensive. Regardless, I have three pairs, and they are the only work pants I have used for over four years, and they still look brand new; it's crazy. How many pairs of work pants do you buy a year? If I had purchased $50 work pants, they would look terrible and wouldn't last very long.

Over the long term, buying the better product will save you a surprising amount of money. This is one of those secret non-identifiable savings because you will not physically see the savings on a per-transaction basis. Over that year, if you are tracking your money at a detailed level, like I do and you should, you will find that you are starting to spend less money in certain categories: *Oh, I didn't have to buy tires again; I didn't have to buy work pants again or another pair of shoes.* It adds up a lot faster than you'd think. If you are trying to save money by purchasing lower-quality items because you don't have the money now, save up until you can buy quality, or you will be wasting your money.

Don't Be Fooled by the Packaging

Don't ever be fooled by how a product is packaged. Why do some products have a wide range of prices for, seemingly, the same thing? When looking at a range of products like this, which one actually makes sense to buy? This question reminds me of when I was at Home Depot looking into buying a new drill. They have drills that cost $40 to $400. I'm not telling you to buy the $400 dollar drill, but I suspect that drill is probably made of better materials and will probably last a lot longer, although it's hard to justify that higher price. When I'm in a situation with a high price spread, I always spend right in the middle of the price range. Never buy the cheapest product in this category because it's produced with inferior quality and is a trap for people who think they are saving money. The expensive one, in this example, is probably a commercial grade product, which most people don't need. Since they look the same, it is hard not to buy the cheapest one, but trust me, the internal components are much different, and that cheap drill will send you back to the hardware store soon to purchase another one.

Another place to really turn your value detector on is at the grocery store. Always check out the per-unit price on the shelf signs, and never let your mind be tricked by packaging. Many times, purchasing a larger quantity of an item will have a lower price per unit. It hurts, initially, to buy in bulk, but you will end up saving over the long term. Aluminum foil is the biggest culprit of all. The packaging is always exactly the same, but the prices are vastly different. If you focus on the per-unit price, one roll can cost twice as much as another on a per-unit basis. The common shopper will just grab the cheap one and be on their way. Little do they know they just paid 100% more per unit for the same product. I look at products like this and laugh; the companies want you to buy the cheaper one because they make double the profit. Next time you are at the store, check out the price per unit. Buy the product with the lowest per unit cost and ignore the total cost. This may hurt up front because it can cost you more, but over time you will start to see a lot of savings from this one change in buying behavior.

Buy at the Right Time

"Whether we're talking about stocks or socks, I like to buy quality merchandise when it's marked down."

—Warren Buffet

If you are buying a product, would you rather pay more or less? That is a really tough question, but I bet you would choose to pay less. When planning your purchases to achieve this; timing is everything. Certain things are always cheaper at certain times in the year. Say you want to take a weekend trip. Rather than flying out on Friday and coming home Sunday like nearly everyone else does, fly out on Saturday and come home Monday night (or other off days), and it will be a win-win. First, flying on less-travelled days is cheaper because most people aren't flying; and places are not as crowded on Mondays because most people are at work. You can avoid crowds *and* save money. Flights are typically cheaper on Tuesdays, and it's usually cheaper to buy a flight two to three months in advance.[16]

---

16 CheapAir.com, https://www.cheapair.com/blog/when-to-buy-airline-tickets-based-on-1-5-billion-airfares/.

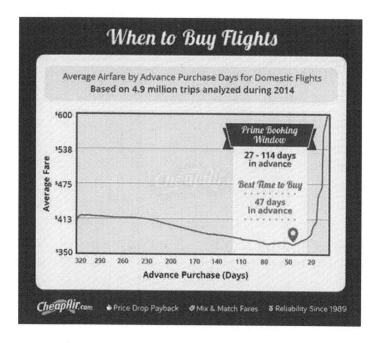

When to Buy Flights

Average Airfare by Advance Purchase Days for Domestic Flights
Based on 4.9 million trips analyzed during 2014

Prime Booking Window

27 - 114 days in advance

Best Time to Buy

47 days in advance

Advance Purchase (Days)

CheapAir.com ◆ Price Drop Payback ✓ Mix & Match Fares 🕙 Reliability Since 1989

Do your research to understand when it's best to plan and pay for the trip.

What happens when your fridge is on the fritz? Don't wait until you absolutely need one, look for the annual or semiannual sales that usually run over Labor Day or Memorial Day. Buy the refrigerator you want, and then donate the other one for a tax write-off. Win-win. You will have already picked out the fridge you want, so just wait until those sales happen and you get a discount. Why pay more?

Do you need sporting equipment? Maybe a new snowboard or your son needs football pads. Always buy that type of gear in the off season. For example, I love to snowboard, and the only time I ever buy new gear is right after the ski season ends. Because guess what? All the companies increase their prices during the winter because people purchase what they will use that instant, no matter the price. When the snow melts, so does the demand for these products.

Do you want a road or mountain bike? Buy a bike in the dead of winter. Convertible? Also buy this in the winter. How about those new snow boots? Buy those in the summer. You get the point. If you ever are buying a product that is utilized during a certain season, buy it during the off-season to save money.

Holiday Deals

Feeling festive for the holiday season? Buy your decorations the day after the holiday is over. Have you ever seen what Christmas lights cost on December 1st compared to December 31st? It is a very big difference. Don't get caught up in the hype, and learn to plan ahead. If you are scrambling to buy decorations before Christmas, you will end up paying five times more for them when they are in demand. We are planning to update our Christmas decorations this year, and we are going to start shopping on December 26th.

How about car shopping? Buy a used car at the end of the month. The dealer will have monthly sales targets to hit, so you will likely pay less as a result. You should also buy at the beginning of the year. This is because the car dealers need to move the prior year's "new" inventory to make way for the upcoming year's "new" inventory. They are going to have a lot of great deals because they need to sell a lot of new cars. But, we are not buying new cars? Good catch! If they are selling a lot of new cars, do you know what that means for the used-car market? Everyone buying a new car will be trading in their older cars to "take advantage" of the deals they can get on new cars at year end (don't be fooled, it's impossible to get a good deal on a new car.) Due to the higher volume of people trading in their used cars for a new one, the dealers will have a large spike in the inventory of used cars at the start of the year. Take advantage of this timing.

At the beginning of the year, people are usually trying to recover financially from the holiday season, and the other half just bought a new car, so they are recovering too. Additionally, everyone is waiting for their tax refunds around this time. This is the perfect recipe for a deal: car dealers have a lot of used cars and no one to buy them. Take advantage of the seasonality. If you are really financially fit you will buy that used car in January or February, and instead of trading in your current car, you will hold it until late February or early March, when everyone is getting their tax refunds, and sell it when people are flush with money again. Buy low and sell high. This type of behavior can save you thousands of dollars on a transaction like this.

Travel Deals

Don't be the peak-season junkie: travel during the off season to get more bang for your buck. Two things I dislike are paying more for the same experience and being in crowded places, which is the main reason I love traveling during the off season. There are fewer people at your travel destination, and everything is considerably less expensive when compared to the peak season.

One reason many people choose to travel during peak times is related to holiday schedules at work and at school. Instead of taking five days off work, people will travel over Labor Day weekend, for example, so they only have to take four days off work. Genius? Not really. You will end up paying twice as much for everything because you are just running with the pack. Its simple supply and demand. Check any hotel pricing during peak holiday times. If you want what everyone else wants, when every else wants it, you will pay more. Rather than fighting the crowds and the inflated prices, just take an extra day off work and travel at another time. Most people can squeeze in one extra day off, and it will be so worth it as you can enjoy your vacation away from the masses and probably save enough to take a second trip later that year.

CHAPTER 12

How to Think About Insurance and Warranties

Insurance is a necessity, but I limit the amount of insurance I carry on my assets. When I talk about insurance, I'm also including product warranties in that category. Whether it's a video game or a season pass to your local ski resort, there's an optional insurance/warranty product to go along with your purchase. Let me be the first to tell you that warranties are very profitable, high-margin products for the *companies*; the warranty products are far more valuable to *them*, not to you. Do you think they would sell an insurance product or warranty on an item if they lost money on it? No! Think about how many times you have used an insurance product. If you are like me, it's rarely or never. One thing that drives me nuts about that industry is they are selling to people based on fear.

Self-Insure

I was buying a car once and they were trying to sell me a warranty package that would cost almost $4,800. The guy behind the counter said, "What if your transmission falls out on your way home? This warranty would pay for itself." I looked at the guy, pretty angry with how he was trying to sell me this product, and asked him, "How often have you had to replace a transmission in your car?"

Maybe I caught him off guard, because he stumbled over his words a little, which made me laugh, and he replied, "I have not had to replace a transmission, but there is a chance." This made me think of the quote from *Dumb and Dumber* when Jim Carey was given odds of one million to one, he replied, "So you're saying I have a chance?" You do have a chance, but the odds are not in your favor.

The way I see it, if the odds are in my favor that my car's transmission or other expensive component's won't break, why would I pay for a warranty that costs the same as a new transmission? Buying the warranty guarantees that I will spend $4,800 on car repairs, and have no upside for any savings if my car doesn't need repairs. By denying this warranty/insurance, at least I have the upside of saving $4,800. Odds are in your favor that you will not spend more than the warranty costs, or else the companies providing those warranties would go out of business. Do you think these companies lose money on these products? No! They make loads of money on these products. If the companies are making a lot of money on those products, then my odds are better if I don't buy it. It's like a casino, the only reason they offer you the different types of gambling products is because they are guaranteed to make money on them. The odds always favor the house, *always*. Companies that offer warranties/insurance on products are like the casinos, and the house always wins. I challenge you to think this way the next time you are offered a warranty on a product.

Top Tip: Instead of buying a warranty, just keep a savings account labeled "Warranty." Turn down all warranties, and deposit what those warranties would have cost into your new savings account. If you end up having to pay to repair or replace the product, take the money out of this account. Chances are this account will have zero withdrawals. This is called self-insurance, because you are now the insurance company.

Auto Insurance and Home Insurance

I'm paying for insurance, but I'm penalized for taking out a claim? This is maddening. I set my deductibles high, because the only way I would ever make an auto claim is if I had a significant accident. Why? Because when you file a claim, the insurance companies increase your premiums for the next couple of years as a way to recoup the costs associated with claims. If they are going to increase the amount of your premiums for the next couple years, it only makes sense to file an insurance claim if the claim is for a large dollar amount.

Why not set your deductible higher and pay lower premiums each month? You should. Here's an example. Say you backed into a pole when reversing out of your driveway. The cost to repair your car is $1,500. You can make an insurance claim, but that would not be a smart idea. The increase in your premiums over the next few years will cost you much more than it would have cost to just pay for the claim out of pocket. Let's say a tree fell on your car and it was totaled. In this case, it makes sense to file a claim because the increase in your future premiums will be significantly less than the loss on the car. The ideal deductible to have on your insurance is a balancing act. If you don't have the ability financially to come up with a high deductible when you have to, then it doesn't make sense to set it high. Strive to build up a savings account and label it "insurance deductible." Deposit the amount of your deducible into that account. Use this account to help pay for small damages along the way, and if something major happens, you will have the money ready to pay your deductible.

Also, if possible, change your deductible with the season if you have seasonal weather. I faced this last summer and ended up saving myself a lot of money. I live in Colorado, and it hails frequently in the summer. The insurance companies consider hail an "act of God," which means it's not in your control, and your premiums won't increase if you have a claim. Last summer I specifically purchased a commuter car to reduce the miles driven on my Ford Raptor. This also ensured my baby was safe from hail as it sat in my home's garage, since we don't have covered parking at my office. I usually keep my deductibles at around $2,500. Since it hails a lot here, I decided to reduce my deductible to $500 on the car I purchased. This worked out really well, I kid you not, the next day the clouds opened up and dropped large hail pellets leaving countless dents on my commuter car. Since I dropped my deducible from $2,500 to $500, $500 was all I had to pay. I saved $2,000 dollars simply by adjusting my deductible for seasonality. The company I used to fix the hail damage was advertising that they would cover $400 of your deductible if you chose them to fix your car. The hail damage ended up costing me $100, and the insurance company had to pay $5,000.

Home insurance works in exactly the same way. Set your deductible's high, enjoy the lower premiums, and only file a claim if the cost to repair outweighs the estimated increase in your premiums over the next few years. Filing a claim will often cost you more money down the road, unless that claim is for a large amount.

To sum up this section, buying warranties just guarantees that these products will cost you extra money. Set your deductibles high on insurance products and enjoy lower premiums. I like to gamble when the odds are in my favor, so I don't pay for warranties, and I set my deductibles high.

CHAPTER 13

Investing Your Money

The next step on the road to financial fitness is investing your money. I will reiterate that I'm not a financial advisor. If you are new to investing, speak to a financial advisor to determine your investment priorities and goals. In this chapter we will talk about what you need to accomplish before you invest, target savings rates, retirement planning, and when it makes sense to pay down your mortgage.

Before you think about investing, you need to be debt free, excluding your mortgage, and have three-to-six months of safety net savings. The only exception to this rule is contributing to your company-sponsored retirement plan to receive the maximum match, even if you have debt. This is a guaranteed 100% return on your money, so never pass this up. No other investment will fetch a 100% return.

People often think the only way to grow their money is through traditional investing. But let's take a step back for a second. The goal is building wealth, right? After reading about how a balance sheet works, we now know of two ways to build your wealth. One way is to invest your money and make a return as it grows. The other way is to *reduce your liabilities*. Both of these will increase wealth. Paying down your debt is just as much of an investment as traditional investing. We have talked about the average return of the stock market in this book, but it's important to note, this is the *average*. Some years the stock market will return a loss, and some years it will return a gain. When you invest money, you could lose it, but over the long term, it's a great move with your money.

Now let's talk about paying down debt. Your debt is a 100% guaranteed *return* on investment. If you have debt with an interest rate of 7%, then every dollar you reduce that debt by will save you from paying 7% in interest. If you really want to grow your net worth, start by reducing your debt first and make that guaranteed rate of return. After you have eliminated your debt (excluding your mortgage) and filled your safety net savings, then you can start investing your money in a traditional fashion.

How to Save Wisely

As I said earlier, plan to save 15% of your income. Fifteen percent is the minimum, and obviously there is no maximum. If you cannot save 15% of your income, then you are probably overspending in other areas. Making more money rarely solves that issue because, most of the time, people will just spend more if they have more. Structure your life so you can afford to save 15%. If you don't, you will not be able to afford much later in life. If you do have debt, then this 15% savings goes toward paying down your debt. Once the debt is paid off, funnel this 15% into building your three-to-six months of safety net savings. After that is done, your 15% savings will be directed toward investing or paying off your mortgage. We will dive into this shortly.

Think Long-Term

With both saving and investing, make sure you are always thinking long-term. It is ideal to invest for at least ten years. At a minimum, you should hold all investments for at least one year because otherwise you will pay short-term capital gains tax on profits made on short-term investments. Capital gains tax is 35% on short-term versus 15% on long-term investments. Long-term investments are classified as investments held for over a year. With that said, if you are putting money into an investment, it is best to have a ten-year time horizon to make sure you weather out the inevitable stock market fluctuations.

Having your three-to-six months of safety net savings before you invest is critical. Use your safety net savings for emergencies, and never touch your investment account. The last thing you want is to experience a market crash and be forced to liquidate your investments.

Investing 101

What should you invest in? Again, speak to a reputable financial advisor who will be able to tailor a plan for your unique situation and goals. I can tell you that I invest in low-cost mutual funds and in retirement target funds through my employer's 401(k) plan. I track my investment performance against the S&P 500 return. As long as I'm in the ballpark for returns on the S&P 500, then I'm good with the return I'm earning. If there is one thing I know about investing in general, the lower-fee funds will render the highest and most consistent returns over time. High fees do not necessary mean large returns.

To make this point clear, Warren Buffet once made a $1 million bet with a hedge fund manager on whether investing money in the S&P 500 would render a higher return over the following ten years vs. a basket of funds hand-picked by that hedge fund manager. Guess who won? Over that ten-year period, the S&P 500 increased by almost 136% percent, while the hedge fund manager's basket of funds only increased by 36%. Moral of the story: don't let high fees make you think high returns.

When should you invest? Never invest large chunks of your money at one time because it is impossible to time the market. First, figure out how much you want to invest during that year, and make those investments on a consistent basis (for example, buying every other Friday). This will help smooth out market activity and render a higher return over time vs. trying to predict market fluctuations. The key to investing is consistency. Buying at consistent intervals and committing to your strategy takes emotion out of the investment equation.

Another item to note is that the risk of your investments should decrease as you get closer to retirement—whatever age that is for you. I also would never actively day trade stocks unless you understand how to value companies, which only applies to a small percentage of people.

This is good advice because, all too often, people will sell when the market is down out of fear of losing more, or sell when the market is going up out of fear that the market may go back down. The key to investing is consistency. Plan to buy a little often, and never change your strategy based on market volatility. Don't let any late-night TV commercial trick you into thinking you can make a boatload of money in a short period of time. If you cannot handle the behavioral side of investing, then it would be best to let the investment professionals handle your money.

Retirement Accounts

One of the biggest questions I am asked by those seeking advice is, "How much should I be contributing to my retirement account?" If you start contributing early and consistently, you will not have to contribute as much as you would if you start later. Time is your best friend with investments. If you are asking that question in your late forties, the answer is, "As much as possible." Why? There is this little principal called compound interest that really helps take your contributions to the next level. The next chapter delves into the benefits of compound interest. You know what makes millionaires? Two things: time and compound interest.

Let's focus on the different options at a high level. As far as contributions go, I believe you should target 15% of your income into retirement accounts *after* your debt is paid off and you have three-to-six months of safety net savings. Because this money is locked up until you are over the age of fifty-nine, you don't want to contribute more than you need to either. For most people, this is not something to be concerned about. I challenge you to either speak to a financial advisor or Google a "retirement calculator." A retirement calculator will help you understand how much money you need invested at different stages of your life to hit "your number."

Roth Versus Traditional Individual Retirement Accounts (IRAs) and 401(k)s

The primary difference between a Roth and a Traditional retirement account is the tax implications. With a Roth account, you pay taxes on the money *before* it is invested and no taxes upon withdrawal after age fifty-nine and one half. All of the interest you earn during that time is tax free. With a Traditional retirement account, you invest the money pretax, meaning before Uncle Sam has taxed it; and the entire account balance (including interest earned) is then taxed upon withdrawal after age fifty-nine and one half.

The amount you contribute to a Traditional account will reduce your taxable income for the current year, but you are taxed upon withdrawal. A Roth is taxed before the money is invested, and not taxed upon withdrawal.

Do you want a tax break now, or do you want a tax break later in life? That is the only question to ask yourself.

Which one is better? The answer is, it depends.

Although contributions to a Roth account don't reduce your taxable income in the current year, you don't have to pay any taxes upon withdrawal, which can be a big perk. Say you're currently in the 20% tax bracket, and when you retire you're in the 30% tax bracket. If you invested in a Roth IRA, you just saved 10% on that money because it was already taxed at 20% when you contributed, and you get to withdraw it tax free. If you think your tax bracket will be higher when you retire, then investing in a Roth is a good hedge. Another really great benefit of a Roth is the financial security of knowing exactly how much money you have to live on. Since the money was already taxed, you have no tax risk later in life. You can plan to use your full balance any way you want because it's already been taxed.

Is one better than the other? Well, if you invest the same amount of money in both types of accounts *and* your tax bracket remains the same, the amount upon withdrawal would be exactly the same. This is really important to note about these accounts. *The only difference is the tax rate.* Do you think your tax rate is higher now, or will it be higher later? That is an impossible question to answer.

What do I personally do? We have a Roth 401(k) and a traditional 401(k) because I want options when I retire. Plus having both gives me the opportunity to manage my taxable income later in life. In years when I have a higher taxable income, I will withdraw from the tax-free Roth account. In years when I have a lower taxable income, I can withdraw from my traditional IRA.

Even if you are struggling financially, find a way to take advantage of a 401(k) match if your company offers this benefit. Would you pass up free money? If you saw $10 on the street, would you pick it up? Of course you would, because free money is the best money, right? I talk to a lot of people who think deferring money into a retirement account is an expense. They tell me, "I need that money this year." They are right that it is an expense, but you are paying yourself, and your company is paying you to do so. A 401(k) match is a guaranteed 100% investment return. I highly doubt you can beat that anywhere else. No matter what, you need to invest at least what your company will match.

This is the tip of the iceberg when talking about retirement accounts and financial planning. My job is to get you to the point where you can invest your extra money. When that happens, make an appointment with a financial advisor.

Paying Down Your Mortgage

This is a highly debated subject. Should I pay down my home mortgage or invest that money? Paying off your mortgage is the pinnacle of financial freedom because you will be knocking out your largest monthly expense. The second you pay off your house and are debt free is the second you could, technically, make minimum wage and survive just fine —with an emphasis on survive, not thrive. The only problem is that the money in your house is "dead money" when compared to other investments because your equity isn't earning money every year.

Well, it is and it isn't. If you don't pay down your mortgage, you'll have to pay interest on your loan balance. Which way should you go? Again, it depends.

You have a guaranteed return on every dollar you use to pay off your mortgage. The "return" you make on that money depends on your interest rate. Every dollar you pay down is a dollar you're not going to have to pay interest on ever again. If your interest rate is 5% and you pay it down, you just reduced a liability by 5% this year, next year, the year after that, etc. You are making 5% on your money because if you didn't pay down that amount, you would be paying 5% on the balance. There are not a lot of investments that have a guaranteed tax-free return. Paying down your mortgage is a guaranteed tax-free return on your money.

When thinking about paying down your house, it comes down to your interest rate on your mortgage versus what you *think* you could make on other investments. Think is a huge variable here, and investments are a game of chance. Obviously, if you knew you could make a guaranteed return of 10% on a certain investment every year and your mortgage interest rate is 5%, it would be foolish to ever pay down a dollar of your mortgage. A world where you are guaranteed to make 10% would be a great world to live in, but unfortunately that is not reality.

First of all, if you are in a position to choose whether to pay down your house or invest extra cash, congratulations, you are in an enviable position. A financially fit person doesn't like debt, but a financially fit person is also about maximizing wealth. My answer to the question of when to pay down your mortgage is: "It all depends on your age."

If you are in your twenties or thirties and have a low mortgage rate, you will most likely earn a higher compounded return on your capital by investing in other assets versus paying down the loan. But that all depends on your risk appetite. Personally, I have a fifteen-year mortgage because I'm a fan of balance. Yes, if I invested every dollar in the market, I would probably have a better chance of making more than my current mortgage interest rate. But having financial freedom is very important to me and paying down your house early is never a bad idea.

If you are over forty, start thinking about using your extra money to pay down your mortgage. By the time you retire, you should plan to have your house paid off. Retirement is the stage in your life when you don't want monthly payments; you worked all your life to enjoy the fruits of your labor, and monthly payments will eat into your life enjoyment. The closer you get to retirement, the more it makes sense to pay down your home aggressively.

Fifteen- or Thirty-Year Mortgage?

The question of whether to have a fifteen- or a thirty-year mortgage. If you can afford it, a fifteen-year mortgage is better in the long term. Yes, a fifteen-year mortgage requires a higher monthly payment, but a lot of it goes to paying down the principal balance of the loan. I like this financing instrument because you pay significantly less interest expense over the term of the loan, and you usually get a discounted interest rate. You will receive a lower interest rate because your investment is lower risk for the bank; they get their money back sooner versus a thirty-year mortgage.

How much interest are you saving with a fifteen-year mortgage? If you have a thirty-year mortgage with a 4% interest rate on a $300,000 house, you will pay 72% of that home's value in interest expense, or $216,000 of interest expense in addition to the $300,000 you initially borrowed. If you have a fifteen-year mortgage with the same 4% interest rate, you will pay only 33% of the home's value, or $100,000 of interest expense. I wanted to show you an example with the same interest rate, but you will typically get around a 0.5% lower rate on a fifteen-year mortgage, so you will end up paying even less than the $100,000 in this example. Apart from saving the interest expense, it's a great tool that will force you to build equity faster in your house, which increases your net worth.

If you have a thirty-year mortgage and tell yourself you will prepay it, you also have the option of not prepaying, so don't fool yourself. If there is anything I have learned in life, it is that something always comes up where you will say, "Oh, it's okay, I will start prepaying next year." This will become a vicious cycle, and you will not end up prepaying as planned. A fifteen-year mortgage requires you to pay that extra amount because it's required by the lender. Think of the price difference between a thirty-year and a fifteen-year mortgage as an investment account. You are investing in real estate. If you are passionate about paying down your house, take out a fifteen-year mortgage. If you want to prepay even more principal, go for it. Do not get a thirty-year mortgage with the thought that you will prepay the loan down to the equivalent of a fifteen-year mortgage, because chances are you won't.

The Cost of Inflation

Everything we talk about below is excluding your three to six months of safety net savings. You must have some money on the side sitting in cash as your safety net. Additional cash sitting in a very low-interest or non-interest bearing account is dead money. If you are not making a decent return on your money, you are losing money due to inflation. Inflation is the increasing price of the regular goods we all buy; reducing the purchasing power of a dollar. Think about this... the price of bread used to be $0.05, and the price of that same loaf of bread today is closer to $4.00. If you are not paying down debt or investing your money, you are losing money. As scary as it may be to invest money, it's important that you don't just leave your extra cash in an account that is not earning interest. Cash sitting in a checking account that is not growing is losing money. If you keep extra savings in a checking account that is not growing, the price of goods you buy every day will increase (due to inflation), but your money won't.

CHAPTER 14

Compound Interest

Who doesn't like free money? How about making money while you sleep, or while participating in the hobbies you enjoy? Yeah, I like that... Tell me more. Let me introduce you to my friend, compound interest. It is just about the best thing in the world. When asked about his secret to becoming wildly successful, Berkshire Hathaway CEO, Warren Buffet was very quick to say, "My wealth has come from a combination of living in America, some lucky genes, and compound interest."

Begin Saving Now to Maximize Compound Interest

The first thing I want to say is that no matter your age or where you are in your life, start saving and investing now. If you can commit to saving a little each month, it will add up faster than you think. Remember, $1 million is the accumulation of one million small decisions each day.

Here is some quick math that will help you understand the power of time and compound interest. At what age do you want to retire or live on passive income? Subtract your current age, and you will come up with a number. Maybe your number is forty, or maybe your number is fifteen. Check the table below to see how much every dollar you invest could be worth by the time you want to use it in retirement. As you can see, time multiplies returns.

Years	Multiplier[1]
5	1.5x
10	2.2x
15	3.2x
20	4.7x
25	6.8x
30	10.1x
35	14.8x
40	21.7x

[1] assmumes 8% average yearly return

If you are a twenty-five-year-old who wants to retire at sixty (meaning thirty-five years to go), buying that $5.00 Starbucks drink is actually costing you $74.00 dollars in retirement savings. It is important to have a balance here; you should enjoy your life and don't need to save every dollar you make. But make sure to keep this in the back of your mind when you are spending instead of saving. If something will cost you 14.8x the sticker price in future dollars, it better bring a lot of value to your life.

A Starbucks is a small dollar amount, and one drink will not limit your savings potential in a material fashion. Let's think about how a large purchase can impact your savings in retirement. Let me paint a picture. You are twenty-five years old, and you really want that amazing new car, and you deserve it because you just got a raise. That cool new car is $40,000. You say you are going to be responsible and pay cash for the car, so you start to save. Instead of saving for retirement, because it's so far away, you stop contributing to your 401(k) and save for the car instead. It takes you three years of saving $13,333 a year to have enough money to purchase the vehicle. You tell yourself after those three years, you will start contributing again. That doesn't seem like a big deal, right? It's smart to buy a car with cash, right? What did that just cost you in potential retirement savings? The answer is...almost $600,000. Crazy right? That $40,000 took you three years to save, so you didn't invest the $13,333 a year you put aside for the car. Let me blow your mind a little more. Say instead of buying the car for $40,000, you take that amount and invest it and continue to invest $13,333 for the following three years. How much would you have in potential retirement savings if you did that? You could have $1,000,000 in your retirement account. Don't let any large purchase derail your savings habits early in life, because if you start early, it doesn't take a lot of savings to have a lot of money and freedom later in life. I always recommend paying cash for everything, but make sure you continue to save and invest. Never put your retirement savings on hold to make luxury purchases.

Here is how I like to think about it, and I will lay out my plan. I like to get deals, so starting to save early is like getting a deal on having a lot of money when I retire. If I begin now, I won't need to put in as much money to have a healthy retirement savings later. My plan is to save enough money by the time I turn forty so that I, technically, will never need to contribute another dollar into my retirement accounts, and will have enough to live well on by the time I turn sixty. However, I will keep contributing, because the tax savings of retirement accounts are amazing, and I obviously won't turn down a 401(k) match.

Retiring As a Millionaire

Do you want a million dollars? Depending on your age, how much would you need to contribute each month to achieve this assuming an average 8% return compounded annually?

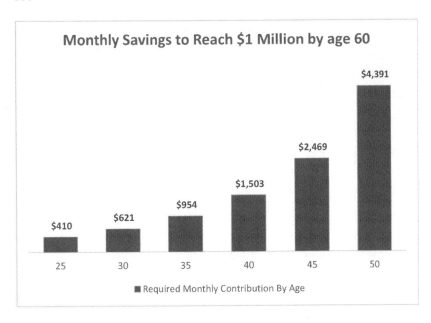

The key is to start now. Look at the chart for a twenty-five-year-old. You only need to save $410 each month. The historical growth rate of the stock market is around 8%, so our estimate is right in line with the average. Boom: $1 million by saving just $410 a month. That's the same amount as a car lease payment; you can certainly save that amount. It doesn't matter how much you make, it matters how much you save. Even if you work at a fast-food restaurant, you can still become a millionaire. On the flip side, if you delay saving, your million dollar goal may slip away. Look at the chart again, if you wait until 50 to start, you have to save $4,400 a month to reach $1 million by age 60. Not many people can save $4,400 a month. Don't let that be your story. Focus today on small wins, because those small wins add up with your friend compound interest.

The Small Things Add Up

Here is a personal example of how doing small things, can end up producing massive results in the long run. I have a large retaining wall in my backyard and noticed one day that it was on the brink of falling over. First thing I did was request a quote for how much it would cost to hire someone to complete the job. That price was almost $15,000—*yikes*. Instead, I did it myself. This retaining wall is over 80 feet long and is 6 feet high. Each cinder block of the wall weighs over 40 pounds, and there were more of them than I could count.

If I only focused on the short term, there is no way I would have been able to rebuild that wall. Because after the first day, I didn't even get the wall completely torn down, and my body ached badly. It took me two weekends with the help of a friend to even get the wall dismantled. Not to mention, all the dirt I had to move afterward by myself; I only had help on demolition day. A 6-foot wall that is 80 feet long holds a lot of dirt, trust me. Just thinking about it actually gives me anxiety. Similar to how you might be thinking right now: *"There is no way I will ever have $1 million."*

However, that is not how I thought about building my wall: I thought that if I just do a little bit, each day, it would get done at some point. At times I would overestimate how much I could get done in the short term, but I never underestimated how much I could get done over the long term. Block by block, day by day, I just did a little bit after work. Whenever I had a little bit of free time, I worked on the wall, whether it was five minutes or twelve hours. When I laid the last brick, even I was shocked at what I was able to accomplish. It took me nearly all summer to complete this job, but this experience taught me that no task is too large. If you take small steps toward something, you can accomplish anything. It just takes dedication, a habit and consistency. I mean $410 dollars can make you a millionaire, and a scrawny 165-pound man (me) can build a massive retaining wall. Persistence renders results.

Ask for a Pay Raise at Work...Often

One last thing I want to add about compound interest is something you may not, initially, think is relevant to the topic, but it is. It's important for your future to renegotiate your salary often. The impact on your salary is compound interest at its finest because a $5 raise today, is a $5 raise every day for the rest of your life. And your next raise is calculated as a percentage increase on what you currently make, and so on and so forth. You are leaving a lot of money on the table if you are not consistently striving for more. It's like a snowball that keeps building.

A small raise will obviously not change your life today but think about this. Every year most companies offer a cost-of-living increase for their employees, so that small raise now has an additional compounding effect because your base wage will be higher each year when they hand out that small cost of living adjustment. It's usually around 2-3%, but that is 2-3% on a higher base wage every year until you retire. Every time you change jobs or get promoted, renegotiate your pay. After you are in a job for a year, have your employer lay out a plan for what it takes to get you to the next level. Attack that plan and do what it takes to get to the next level, execute those steps and document everything. Then next year you will have done everything asked of you, and you will have the proof. Now you can ask for more money. Constantly ask and get those small promotions.

I'll let you in on a little secret. Most promotions and salary increases come as a percentage of what you already make. Companies rarely hand out lump sums of money. Now that you know this, you need to get your pay up as high as possible as quickly as possible. Every wage increase in the future will be calculated off the higher base pay you negotiated today, and therefore be a higher amount than if you had not received that previous increase. This cycle of compounding is continuous throughout your career. Head over to Thirtysomethingmillionaire.com to see how I once gave a PowerPoint presentation in order to get my first promotion.

CHAPTER 15

The Second-Largest Purchase You Will Make in Life, Automobiles

Pop quiz: What type of sale makes the most money for the dealership?

A) Lease

B) Financing

C) Cash purchase

The answer is A. But why does a lease make a dealership more money if it's the lowest monthly payment? A lease payment is lower than financing because when you finance a car, part of your payment is going to principal (meaning, paying down the loan). A lease just means that car is being rented, so the payment is lower, but 100% of that cost is lost to you. When you finance a car, at the end of the term you will own that car, so you can use that money for the next car. In a lease, you never own it, so after the term is up, you have no equity and no car to your name.

Leasing a Car

How does a car lease work? The car companies have teams of employees crunching numbers on the historical depreciation of their vehicles. They are renting this car to you over a fixed duration of miles and years. They want to make sure that at the completion of the lease, they have pocketed more money in payments than the car has depreciated in value. Really, all a lease is doing is paying for the depreciation of the car, plus some extra cash for the car company. If you are leasing, you are, literally, just paying for the amount the car loses in value plus dealership fees.

I love seeing the commercials marketing a lease; I always pause the TV to read the fine print so I can do the math and see how much it is actually costing people. First they quote the monthly payment for the least expensive base model, and the fine print is where the details reside. A payment of $479 dollars a month for a Mercedes doesn't sound horrible; it is, but let's pretend it's not for the sake of this discussion. You might be the envy of the block with the three-pointed star emblem on your hood, but once you start adding options, such as navigation, leather, keyless entry, adjustable seats, etc. that monthly lease payment starts to climb into the $600s. On that three year lease someone would end up paying $21,600. This is bad, but it's about to get worse. The fine print is where you are really taking the financial hit.

That advertisement I was looking at said you have to pay $3,999.99 at signing in addition to a $599.99 dealer fee, plus a $1,599.99 landing fee and a $599.99 vehicle turn-in fee. That is $6,800 for a car you'll never own, and then another $600 a month on top of that for the monthly payments. I don't understand how anyone would be okay spending this kind of money to rent a car. I don't like to even lose one dollar on a car, meanwhile Mercedes is charging a customer close to $30,000 for three years, and you don't even own the car. Why would anyone waste that kind of money? The reason these costs are up front and on the tail-end is because no one would want to pay over $800 a month to rent a car. $600 sounds better, and the buyer will forget about those up-front and tail-end costs. There is no upside to leasing for the consumer, only the dealership. *Fun fact*: Over 50% of Mercedes Benzs are on a lease, BMW ranks at 58%, and 63% of all Infinitis are leased.[17] Now that you know the facts, you can understand that most people driving these brands do not own them and are making a terrible financial mistake by leasing them.

Worst of all, with a lease, you are back at the dealer in three years. Do you think the dealers want this? Yes, because now you are back at the dealer in a position where you need to buy or lease again. Don't ever think they are giving you a good deal on a lease. The car companies did the math before they sold you that lease. It's like a casino: when the house makes the rules, the house always wins. It would not be very smart of them to lose money on every deal. Trust me, they are not.

Financing a Car

The second most expensive way to buy a car is financing. Many car companies offer really low rates and they are stretching out the loans to seven years. A low rate and a long-term loan mean you will have a low monthly payment. A low payment is good, right? No, because the real reason the payment is stretched out longer is so it appears cheaper (because it is on a monthly basis). What you aren't seeing is the higher total cost the dealer is collecting through higher interest and fees. Dealerships do this so you are more willing to buy and the lower payment hides the true impact of the money wasted.

The number-one cost you will face is depreciation. On average, new cars will depreciate more than 40% in the first four years. Depreciation is higher for luxury brands and lower for other brands, but a 40% loss in value is still quite a bit. Many people are so conditioned to paying for something monthly that it never crosses the mind where their money is actually going. You would, however, think differently about this if you'd saved up all the money to purchase a new car with cash, and four years later, the dealership gives you just half of that money back. That is not a good deal.

---

[17] Edmunds.com, "Edmunds Lease Market Report," January 2017, https://dealers.edmunds.com/static/assets/articles/lease-report-jan-2017.pdf.

The second-highest cost you will face is the interest expense. You don't have to be a genius to figure out that the longer you finance something, the more interest you will pay. Everyone knows you will face some depreciation on all cars, but you don't have to waste your money on paying interest. What if they offer 0% financing? That will obviously save you the interest expense, but rationalizing the purchase of a new car because of a low or 0% interest rate is a bad idea. Simply because buying a new car is a bad idea. Don't let this swing your decision making. And, many times, at a 0% interest rate, they charge you a fee up front, so it's not actually 0%. And even if it is, there will definitely be extra costs. Keep reading.

The number-three cost? Extra fees, insurance, and forced warranties.

1. *Extra fees*: Dealers charge up-front fees to finance a car, regardless of the interest rate. There is no such thing as free money. In order to process your loan, you will get hit with a fee, depending on your credit and the dealership. These fees can range from several hundred to several thousand dollars.

2. *GAP insurance*: What is this? This insurance product guarantees that you will be able to pay back the loan if the car is wrecked. The bank/dealer will either force you (or scare you) into purchasing this insurance. Since new cars depreciate at such a rapid rate, the banks want to ensure they will be made whole if you get into an accident and total your car. If you do get in an accident and total your car, chances are high that your car insurance company won't give you enough for your damaged car to cover the remaining balance of your car loan—due to how quickly new cars depreciate. Hence there would be a gap in what you'd owe. GAP insurance pays the bank the difference.

3. Warranties: You already know I don't like warranties, but many dealers require extra warranties if you finance a car to ensure you are able to make your monthly loan payments. If something breaks on the car and you have to pay to get it fixed, you might have trouble coming up with the extra money to make your car payment. They make you pay for

the warranty up front, and paying for warranties is a waste of money.

All of the costs associated with financing, apart from interest, are to ensure the banks are covered by offering you financing on the car in the event something happens to that car. How can you avoid all these fees?

Buying a Car with Cash

The cheapest way to buy a car is with cold, hard cash. You don't have to buy a special warranty, purchase GAP insurance, or pay any of the extra fees associated with leasing or financing. You simply walk into the dealer and pay the price of the car. Plain and simple.

I will take it a step further. The cheapest way to buy is a four-year-old *used* car with cash. That way you get a 40% discount off the retail price. Stop thinking about how expensive something is on a monthly basis. You are buying the same thing, why pay more? It's not complicated.

The Only Guide You Will Ever Need: How to Buy a Used Car

Since a car is the second-most expensive thing a household purchases, let's talk about the best way to purchase one. Did you know cars cost people around $5,000 each year on average? This includes things like maintenance, depreciation, and interest expense. Follow the guide below for all my top tips. I have not spent even one dollar on a car over the past eight years. Let me set the record straight: the cars I've purchased over the years were not free to acquire; they did cost money, but I've managed to sell them for enough to cover all my costs and even make some money on them. I do a ton of research on the car, buy it cheap, sometimes fix a couple things, drive them for eight or so months, and then sell them.

If the average cost of car ownership is $5,000 each year, and I have made all my money back on the cars over the last eight years, I have saved roughly $40,000. That is pretty eye opening, isn't it? $40,000 compounded over thirty years at an 8% interest rate is almost $400,000. What if I did this every year until I was sixty? Saving $5,000 each year, compounded over thirty years at an 8% interest rate is close to $900,000. Wow! I could be a millionaire in retirement just from the savings associated with my car purchasing strategy.

$5,000 is just the average cost of a car annually. A brand-new, fully loaded BMW could cost you $15,000 a year. I don't expect you not to lose money on a car though. A good figure to shoot for is having a car that costs you between $1,500 and $2,500 a year. How do you get the best deal? Let's talk about that.

How to Buy a Used Car: The Ten-Step Guide

I don't like to lose money on automobiles. The way to ensure you don't lose money is to buy a used car at a great price. What is the best way to buy a used car? Over the past eight years, I have bought and sold over twelve cars, and I have not lost a single dollar. How you ask? I follow a detailed car-buying strategy that allows me to identify a great deal on a great car. I call this process "Finding a Unicorn."

1. Don't Buy New

Buying a new car is a guaranteed way to lose a lot of money through depreciation and many other factors that follow.

Did you know:

- New cars can depreciate 30% or more the day you drive them off the lot?
- Deprecation is the highest during the first four years of a car's life?
- Factory warranties often transfer upon sale?
- Sales tax is higher because it's based on the purchase price?
- Registration costs go down as the vehicle ages?
- Insurance costs more for a new car?

Buying new is actually a terrible financial decision. People say they want to buy a new car because used cars require more maintenance. But today's cars are more reliable than ever and can go well over 100,000 miles without any major maintenance. Also, once you drive the car off the lot it's used...it's only new before you drive it off the dealership lot.

2. Determine Your Budget

How much money do you want to spend? Make sure you determine this prior to searching for your car. I urge you to pay cash for your car. It's much easier to save money for a future purchase than to pay for something after you already have it. You are going to have to pay for the car at some point, why not pay less for it with cash up front?

Monthly payments can be a trap because you never understand how much the car actually costs you. The amount of your monthly payment means nothing. Think about the total amount of money you want to spend for the car.

If you must finance the car, though, get preapproved from a bank before you buy, and shoot for a *three-year loan* to minimize the interest expense. I challenge you to pay it down as quickly as possible, and after you own the car, continue contributing that "payment" into a savings account for your next car. If you continue this habit, you will be able to pay cash for your next car, your car after that, and your car after that.

3. Picking the Car

Now that the boring stuff is out of the way, let's dive into the art of finding a great used car and getting a great deal on that vehicle.

Research, Research, Research

You need to have every decision made before you step foot on a dealer lot. Sites like Kelly Blue Book, Cars.com, Auto Trader, and True Car are all great ways to see what others are paying for the exact car you are looking at. Don't limit your search to cars that are near you. Take a look at cars out of state and find ones that are good value at highly rated dealerships. The best deal on a car might not be in your backyard.

Print out the page, along with an online valuation (Kelly Blue Book or True Car), and head into the dealer with a price you are willing to pay for the car you want. Don't let the high-pressure sales tactics get to you; have your number and do not budge, no matter what. The salesman is not your friend, and they don't really care about you. No one has your best interest in mind but you. If you are buying out of state, take the same steps before you go to buy the car. When buying out of state, you may have to complete the sale over the phone if the dealership is too far away.

Top Tip: Find cars in places with a low population or that are outside of a city center. Cars for sale in these areas typically sell for less than in a city because the demand is less. I also like to buy cars in January or October. The peak buying times are the end of the year and when people get their tax refund. The prices of cars during those times reflect that demand.

4. The Car's Age

Deprecation trends start to slow down around the three- to four-year mark, so purchase a car that is at least three years old.

Top Tip: When looking for cars, I look at different model years with different mileages to gauge how much each year and mile costs. I like to buy cars with a cult-like following. An example for me is the Subaru WRX. These cars are fantastic at holding value. I have had four of them, and, in total, I have *made* over $3,000. Keep reading, and I will explain how.

If you look at the depreciation curve of most cars, it starts to level out after four years. This means that a car loses a significant amount of value during the first three to four years and doesn't lose as much value after that. That is when you want to buy.

5. Mileage: When Does It Have Too Many Miles?

This all depends on the car. The maintenance a Rolls Royce would require at 100,000 miles is far different than the maintenance a Toyota Camry would require with the same mileage.

My mileage strategy is to look at the price of the car I want to purchase with several different mileages, and pay attention to the effect the mileage has on the price. A pattern will start to develop. You will notice a point where further increases in mileage do not materially change the price of a vehicle. That is your buying window for mileage.

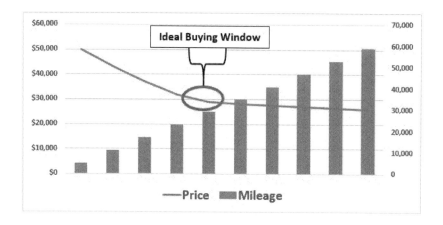

I typically buy cars between 35,000 and 50,000 miles. I never keep cars for too long, and I know the price doesn't usually change much until after the 80,000 mile mark. If you can find a good deal, you can typically drive these cars for a year or two and will not lose a material amount of money when you sell them.

6. Number of Owners

You want a one owner car. It's much easier to sell a car if you can tell the next person buying it that you bought the car from the original owner; it sounds better than saying it's a "two-owner car," right? Cars with many owners are usually a red flag. Why didn't anyone want to keep the car? Go for a single-owner car if possible, or if the car has had multiple owners, make sure each owner had it for at least two years.

7. Vehicle History Report

These come from sites like CarFax and AutoCheck. When buying from a dealer, they will usually give you this report for free, and they are often available online to check out prior to going into the dealership. You need to review the history report, so run one for yourself or be sure to request it if it's not provided.

When buying from a private party, you will typically have to buy the report. They cost around $40, and it's worth the money to ensure there have been no major issues with the car. All you need is the VIN number to pull this report. Don't know where to find the VIN number? From the outside of the vehicle on the driver's side, look at the corner of the windshield where it meets the hood. Or, open the driver's side door and look near the latch. It should be in both of these locations.

Understanding a Car-History Report

Study this report and look at the maintenance history. I like to see a car that was taken in for service every 3,000 to 6,000 miles. A great report will show a car going into the authorized dealer at regular intervals. This is important because it shows that the person took proper care of the car, which will tell you a lot about the past owner(s). Someone who takes a car in for regular maintenance cares about their car.

8. Tires

Always look at the condition of the tires. If you spot a car that is priced right, but the tires are bald, offer $600 dollars lower than the listed price so you can buy new tires. This is a cost sellers will try and pass along. If the tires are bald, your chances of having to buy new tires are 100%. No matter what, you will have to buy tires and this is a large investment in a car.

9. My Biggest Secret: Run a Used-Car Check and Save Thousands

When you buy your used car, have a franchised reputable car dealer conduct a "used-car check." For example, if you're looking to buy a Ford, bring it to a Ford dealer for their used car check. This is usually a 150-point inspection in which they run through the entire car and let you know the condition of all the items inspected. They usually cost around $150 and are well worth the money.

First, you will know the exact condition of the car. Second, you can negotiate the price down and make that $150 back plus potentially much, much more.

If something major is discovered, then either have the seller fix it or give you the money to fix it. If the seller won't fix the vehicle or lower the price, walk away. It's pretty simple. I do this every time; it's much cheaper than buying an extended warranty on the vehicle, and I know up front if it has any issues. Do you want to know the real reason I do this? To lower the asking price on the car...you kill two birds with one stone. Have you ever taken your car to a dealer and had them not find something wrong with it? Probably not; there is always something they can fix. When you are buying a used car, you will have the leverage to lower the price once they see that an authorized dealer found some issues.

Top Tip: I always ask that the seller take the price of what the dealer quoted for the repair off the asking price. After I acquire the car, I try to personally fix all the issues that the used car check uncovered, without paying dealer prices. I can usually do the job and spend about one fourth of the quoted price from the service department at the dealership—or what I refer to as the "stealership."

10. Understand the Total Cost of the Car

The total cost includes the sticker price plus all other taxes and fees. Here are some of the taxes and fees you need to think about:

- Sales tax (sales tax = price of car times the sales tax percentage where you live)
- Dealer fees
- Handling charges
- Paperwork charges and any other miscellaneous charges that dealership requires
- Registration fees to get your plates (The price of your registration will depend on the year of your car)
- Insurance
- Interest on your loan if you are financing the car and any associated loan-origination fees

And that's it. If you follow these ten steps, you are guaranteed to walk away saving money and getting a great car.

Buy from a Private Party or a Dealer?

If you don't know much about cars, I recommend buying a car from a reputable dealer. If you want to buy from a private party, do so, but be sure to have a reputable dealer run a used-car check so you can find out its actual condition. On average, you can save from $1,000 to $2,000 on an automobile when buying from a private party. The cars are usually cheaper because it's riskier than buying from a dealer. When a dealer gets a car, they will not put that car on the lot for sale until they've checked it out. A person selling privately might just be trying to get rid of a car because they know a lot of maintenance is just around the corner. Remember, there are some shady people who will try to sell you a car that needs maintenance and tires. Seems like a great deal until you have to do the maintenance and buy tires.

How to get around this? Pull a vehicle history report and see how the car was serviced and pay for a used car check from a reputable dealer. If both reports come back healthy and the car looks well taken care of, pull the trigger!

Sell Your Car Privately or Trade It in?

The main thing you need to keep in mind is sales tax. You may be able to get more for your car on the private market, but you still need to factor in how much of a discount you would get in the form of a sales-tax reduction on your next car if you trade it in to the dealer. This savings is calculated by trade-in value multiplied by the sales-tax percentage. Consider this example: you buy a car that costs $20,000, and the sales tax rate is 8%. That means you will have to pay $1,600 in sales tax if you are buying the car *without* trading in your current car.

If you trade in your current car and the dealer gives you $10,000 on the trade, you will now only have to pay sales tax of $800, or half of the sales tax since the sale is now $10,000 rather than $20,000. You are saving $800 dollars in the form of a sales-tax reduction. The actual trade-in value of your car to that dealer is $10,800. This is your benchmark on deciding if you want to sell it privately or not. You'll need to make more than $10,800.

If you can get more than $10,800 on the private market, it may be worth your while to sell it on your own. Most of the time, you can sell it for much more because the dealers do this as a business, so they have to buy very low. It's up to you and how much you think your time is worth. I personally never trade in my cars. I get on average around $2,000 more selling them on my own.

If you do decide to sell privately, take high-quality pictures of the car and post the price for at least $500 more than you actually want to collect for the vehicle to leave some haggle room. Pictures of a spotless vehicle that is detailed to perfection are worth around $1,000...so clean your car, and make the pictures look amazing. When it comes time to do the deal, be willing to take $500 off. If you work with the buyer on price, they will think they are getting the upper hand in the deal, but since you have it built into the deal, it's a win win for everyone. They will think they are working you and getting a deal, but in reality, you just got the price you wanted.

CHAPTER 16

How Your Home Affects Your Net Worth

A home is, by far, the biggest purchase you will make in your life. The real danger about this purchase is that there is a lot of emotion involved. Like my dad always said, "Once you fall emotionally in love with something you want to buy, walk away, because you will pay too much."

There are both pros and cons to owning a house. A home is a great way to build wealth and be in charge of your own destiny. As a renter, you have no control over rent prices. If your landlord decides they want to increase rent, you have no choice but to pay more for the same place or move. With a house, you lock in a payment and your payment never changes. That is until your home is paid off, then your payment changes to $0.

On the flip side, as a renter, you never have to worry about a water heater going out, the roof needing to be repaired, or spending your weekends doing home-improvement chores (landscaping, I'm looking at you). Over the long-term, owning a home is much cheaper and comes with many other intrinsic benefits as well. This all hinges on one factor: you must buy the home you can afford. If you buy a home that is out of your league, it will cost you much more than renting your entire life, and can destroy your net worth.

This is a massive decision, and buying a home is not always the correct decision. There are many factors you should consider before signing the dotted line. I want to walk you through the basics of buying a home, and also educate you on what to think about when you are selling a home. Let's start with buying.

The Home Purchase

"Only buy something that you'd be perfectly happy to hold if the market shut down for ten years."

—Warren Buffet

First, determine exactly why you want to buy a home. It is a good decision if the home is a long-term purchase, but if you can't see yourself living in that house for ten years, buying might not be the best choice. If you want to buy a house because you think it's cheaper than renting and believe that renting is a waste of money, though, be careful; it's not always cheaper.

If you buy a house that is way out of your price range, you could end up paying more in interest, maintenance, property taxes, insurance, etc. versus paying rent. Another huge thing people say is that interest is a great tax write-off. Write-offs are great, but not spending money on interest is even better. Now that the President adjusted the tax deductions, you will most likely take the standard tax deduction versus itemizing deductions. What does this mean? It means you will no longer write-off the interest from a mortgage because the standard deduction will most likely be higher. The government created the perception that having a lot of interest expense was good because you got a write-off. Having a large write-off just means you are spending a lot of money, so the fact that you can write something off should never be a large factor in your decision making, and now it's not as applicable. Last year I didn't write off my interest because the standard deduction was much greater.

How Much Home Can You Afford?

Since a home is most likely the largest purchase you will make in your life, it's necessary to make an educated choice about your budget. Don't let the banks dictate your budget for a home. Financial institutions will approve you for over 40% of your debt-to-income ratio (debt to income = monthly gross income/total $ amount of debt payments). The higher your debt-to-income is on a home, the more life experiences you will have to limit as you try to make those monthly payments. You don't want to be "house poor," you want to be "life rich." Your target on a thirty-year mortgage should be around 30% of your *take-home pay* (not your gross pay). Your take-home pay is the dollar amount that goes into your bank account *after* taxes and the 15% you put into savings.

Let's break this down.

	$'s	% of Gross
Gross Income	100,000	100%
Taxes	16,898	17%
Savings	15,000	15%
Take Home Pay	**68,102**	**68%**
Mortgage (30% of Take Home Pay)	20,431	20%
Divide by 12 to get payment target	*1,703*	
Remaining Income	**47,671**	**48%**

It's key to have as much remaining income as possible to give you a fighting chance to pay cash for all the other items life throws at you, without having to acquire debt. Think cars, travel, home maintenance, home upgrades; the list goes on. If your mortgage is too expensive, you will have to limit all other areas in your life. All you will be able to do is sit inside your house because activities cost money and you would not be able to afford them. Too much house often leads to an individual financing cars and running credit card balances, because they simply cannot get ahead due to the large overhang of their monthly mortgage payment.

Getting What You Want

You want to spend the least possible, but it's also important to buy what you want. The last thing you want to do is buy a cheaper house because it fits your budget just to sell it in a couple years. The way I look at purchases is that if you are spending more than $1,000 on something, you should get what you want. When looking for a home, it's important to spend within your budget, but it's also important you get what you want. If what you want is more than you are willing to spend, then wait and buy it when you have the money. Owning real estate for a short period of time opens the door to financial risk and involves high transaction costs.

With real estate, many factors are out of your control. If you buy a house with the mindset that you will just keep it for a few years until you are making more money, then you will sell it to buy what you really want, that is a bad idea and the wrong mindset. During that time, your house could increase or decrease in value; interest rates could increase, but they could also go down; you could be faced with a large expense, such as fixing the roof; or maybe everything remains the same. Yes, there are many unknowns, but the only known is that you will spend quite a bit of money on real estate transaction costs. Most people overlook this fact. Don't be fooled; selling real estate could cost you 6% of the home's value, which includes the 3% commission to the buyer's real estate agent and another 3% commission to the seller's real estate agent. If you have a home worth $400,000 dollars, you could pay upwards of $24,000 to sell it. That is why it pays to wait and get what you want.

If you "have" to get a house now, rather than waiting for the house you want, it will cost you more money, which does nothing but compromise your efforts to get into the home you truly want. I'm *not* telling you to go out and buy that $5 million home of your dreams; you have to be realistic. I am saying that if you are only buying because you hear that renting is bad, you need to understand there is a lot to think about before you make this decision.

This concept is very relevant to first-time home buyers. If you are a first-time home buyer, you are probably early in your career, and you should see a good increase in your salary over the next few years. Waiting to get what you want, rather than settling for less, is the way to go. Don't worry if others are buying homes before you; buy when it makes sense for you. Life is not a sprint.

Run the Analysis

A house is a great tool to build wealth...or destroy it. Let's explore why having a mortgage may be helpful, and next we will explore how it could be harmful to your net worth if you approach home buying incorrectly.

If you are looking at a home, get the following statistics:

- Average annual cost of interest expense (take the total cost of interest expense over the life of the loan, divided by the term (years) of the loan
- Annual mortgage insurance (you should avoid this)
- Annual property taxes
- Annual homeowner's association (HOA) dues, if applicable
- 0.5% of the home's value for maintenance costs
- Incremental utilities expense (water, heat, electricity, sewer, etc.)

You will notice I'm not including the amount you are paying every month that is going to principal. This was intentional because that cost is not lost to you. You will build equity, which adds to your net worth. All the other costs listed negatively affect your net worth. We want to calculate an apples-to-apples comparison for owning versus renting.

Add up these costs and compare the total to your rent. You will come up with an amount that is either higher or lower than your current rent. It's not about which is cheaper, it's really about understanding the associated costs. Head over to thirtysomethingmillionaire.com for your free template to conduct this rent vs. buy analysis. Running this analysis will help you understand the cost of owning the home you are looking to purchase. Should you get a fifteen-year mortgage or a thirty-year mortgage? As I said earlier, I always recommend a fifteen-year mortgage. Apart from saving you a lot in interest expense, this tool forces you to build equity in your house faster, which will help you build your net worth.

Home Renovation

Renovating your house to "increase the value" is not always a smart investment. Unless you are buying a fixer-upper, avoid thinking about renovations as an investment. The only exception is if you are absolutely certain that the changes you make to your house will be worth the money you put into the project.

Here is an example. We have a very large dog who we love so much, but he has destroyed the hardwood floors in our house. They are real wood, so I can always have them refinished. Hiring someone would probably cost between $3,000 and $6,000. If I sold my home right now, the buyer would probably request I refinish my badly worn hardwood floors or request I take the cost to refinish them off the purchase price. If I fix the floors, the money will go back into my home; however, I only plan to fix everything in my house the day I'm ready to sell. Why wait until I sell it? I will wait because if I fix it today, my dog will ruin it... again. And, I don't want to get hit with that cost twice. The moral of the story is: Don't think your home is an investment that you need to plow your savings into. If you want to upgrade your home, do so, but only after you have no debt (other than a mortgage) and can continue to save 15% of your income.

Hiring a company to redo a perfectly fine kitchen usually fetches a *negative* 20% return. Or said another way: each dollar you spend renovating your kitchen is usually worth around $0.80 after the project is complete, due to high labor costs. You can save money and possibly make a return on your investment if you do it yourself. If you are handy, a DIY (Do-It-Yourself) home renovation is a great way to build wealth, but only after you are debt free, excluding the mortgage, and can continue to save 15% of your income. Unless you are going to flip the house for profit, spending your savings on home renovations is not a smart idea. In retirement, a 401(k) will give you the passive income to live your life; that renovation will not. Get your bases covered on the retirement planning first and foremost.

Be careful when thinking of renovating your home, and don't be shocked if you figure out that your net worth went down after the renovation. The only guaranteed way to increase the equity in your home, which increases your net worth, is to prepay your mortgage.

The True Cost of Selling Your Home

Why are you looking to sell? A valid answer to this question would be things like: we are having another child and need more space; we are moving to a different state; we want to be in a good school district; and things of this nature. The wrong answer would be: we have a bunch of equity and want to capitalize on our home's appreciation.

A prime example of this is the Denver housing market. Over the past five years, home values in Denver have been increasing at an alarming rate, which is great for the balance sheet and net worth. However, I hear people saying they want to capitalize on the equity in their home because they think they will make a bunch of money on the house.

Unless you are moving out of Denver to an area that has really cheap housing prices, you are doing nothing but paying real estate transaction costs. Let me break this down. If your house has gone up in value by say 20%, I bet the house across the street has also gone up by 20%. The people who say, "I want to capitalize on the value of my house," don't understand that the house they are going to buy next also went up by 20%. Your actual gain on selling your home is $0; you are just rolling the equity you have into another place that has increased by the same amount. What you need to understand is this move will actually cost you a lot of money, so instead of the "gain" you think you are getting, you are actually going to record a large loss on your balance sheet.

Let me give you a quick example with numbers. Say you bought your home for $200,000 and today it's worth $300,000. That's great; you are up $100,000 on your house. Now you say, "Let's sell this and we make $100,000!" Slow down, you have to live somewhere, right? Right. Perhaps you found a home that is worth $400,000 that you *love*. And now that you have the equity from your current house, you can afford a down payment on this more expensive house. What you are failing to consider is that at the date you bought your first house, the new house you *love* and want to purchase was only worth $300,000 at that time, and now it's worth $400,000. That house also went up by $100,000. Selling to realize a gain of $100,000 is only paying for a gain that the person in the house you *love* is realizing as well. No difference here so far.

You are forgetting about the real estate transaction costs, not to mention the cost of moving. Remember when you bought your house? Did you pay a real estate transaction fee as the buyer? No, because the *sellers* pay all the real estate transaction costs. Now you are a seller. You have to pay the normal 3% to compensate your listing agent, and you have to pay another 3% to compensate the buyer's real estate agent. Since you are selling your home for $300,000, multiply that by 6% to pay a transaction fee of $18,000. That is the cost of you selling a $300,000 home. The messed up part about all of this is many people only think about things on a monthly payment basis (aka *monthly payment syndrome*). People never see this $18,000 dollars because it gets lost in the transaction and is wrapped into your thirty-year loan, thus you don't notice it on a monthly basis.

For $18,000 I could buy a used sports car and drive it around for a year and probably sell it for the same price. I would much rather do that, but then I love cars and you might not. What would *you* rather spend that $18,000 on?

You now need to pay for your move, or do it yourself which will still cost you a lot of money. And chances are you will want new furniture and other upgrades to your new home. On paper, that $100,000 you think you are making is starting to get used up fast. There are more fees you need to think about. You will now have to take out another loan on the house you love, which will leave you paying closing costs that could amount to over $10,000.

Selling a house is an expensive proposition. Thinking long-term is important for an emotional decision like buying a home. If you are buying a home, have a time horizon of at least ten years. Make sure you understand the total cost of selling before you make that decision.

If you are thinking about selling your home, do the math and understand the wealth impact because it can be huge. That is why you should limit the number of times you move. If you are lucky enough to be in a situation where your house has gone up in value, don't think about "realizing" that gain. It's only a true gain if you sell a home in San Francisco and move to rural Arkansas. Because San Francisco is one of the hottest real estate markets in the county, and well, Arkansas is not.

CHAPTER 17

Social Pressure and Money

Money equals freedom. Say *no* to everything that doesn't enrich your life. I'm not telling you to run around like a spoiled brat, saying no all the time. It's probably the word new parents despise the most. As soon as toddlers learn the word *no*, they have the ability to voice their choices.

No Is a Powerful Word

"No" is probably the most underrated word. As a working adult, you probably want to lean toward saying *yes* more often than not. In most other situations, I personally say *no* a lot. Situations can arise when people, instead of thinking about finances, think about what the other person wants to hear. You make a decision because you are worried about what someone will think of you. But who cares what people think about you? Unless the situation is something that you see value in, you need to start saying *no*.

Example: "Hey a bunch of us are going to Starbucks; want to come?"

You: "Yes." (Wait, I thought this was a section about *no*?) Go ahead and tag along; I don't want you to miss out on a fun social situation, but fill your coffee cup before you leave home and head out to enjoy the time with friends. Again, unless you are a coffee enthusiast and cut back in other areas, this is a great way to save money. Will $5 change your life? No, but this behavior over time will lead to thousands of dollars spent unnecessarily each year, which, for me, translates into a week of travel. I would always rather travel. The memories from coffee don't stick out in my mind a year later but traveling does... Spend the money on what you will remember.

Example: You're out at dinner with friends.

At dinner you order cheaper items off the menu for drinks and food. The couple you are with ordered some fancy wine, appetizers, and expensive entrees. Your server comes to ask how you want the check. The other couple says let's just split it down the middle. No. Don't be afraid to say *no*, because that is not right. If the other couple gives you a weird look, who cares? You really need to learn in life that it doesn't matter what people think about you. Stand up for yourself; the other couple is either in la-la land or wanted expensive food on your dime. It might be awkward, once, but if they are good friends, they won't care, and next time it will be smooth sailing. You are just looking to pay for your fair share, and there is nothing wrong with that.

Going down the road to being financially fit takes some selfish actions. You might not be in the position in your life to pay for other people or to donate money to people. Your savings account is your own personal foundation, so donate to that. Once you are rich later in life, then you can give back and donate. For now, say *no* to anything that doesn't add value to your life.

No, no, no, no, no...

I just love that word and have no problem saying no. I really don't care what people think about me, and I know exactly what I want to do with my money and time. I have caught some people off guard when I just say no. If it's not in my budget, and I don't see value in it, then no thank you, I'm good, I don't want to do that. Or no, you all go ahead, and I will catch up after dinner.

Keeping a journal about every time you felt forced to make a decision because of the people around you can be helpful. Analyze that situation afterward, and ask yourself, "What is the worst thing that could have happened if I'd just said *no*?" Someone might think you are poor? Doesn't matter; stick to your individual plan that works best for *you*.

At the end of the day, this is what most people will say about you. "I respect him/her because they know what they want." I used to be teased about

THIRTY SOMETHING MILLIONAIRE • 165

my frugal money habits, now all my friends pull me aside and ask how they can maximize their lives and still thrive financially. When I'm out at dinner with a friend and our bill comes from the bartender and mine is $15 for the night and his is $60, I'm always asked, "How did you do that?"

I tell them, "I asked which beers were on happy hour or special and ordered those all night." How much more fun do you have drinking those expensive beers? The expensive beers are not what you are out for; it's spending time with your friends. The next time I see that person out, I usually see them checking out the happy hour menu, and I love seeing that. If you go out once a week and are able to save like that, drum roll please... That is $720 buckarooskis back in your pocket for the year. Make that change with everything you do, and you will start to see some serious changes in your cash flow.

Keeping up with the Joneses

(Perception Versus Reality)

"Too many people spend money they haven't earned to buy things they don't want, to impress people they don't like."

—Will Rogers

Be yourself. Why are you trying to impress other people? Remember, perception is not reality. Some of the most annoying people are the ones who always try to one-up everything you do. You just got new golf clubs? They just got the newest and most technically advanced golf clubs. You just bought a car? They also bought a car, but it is one model year newer than yours. Yeah, no one likes those people. They are the ones who are always trying to "Keep up with the Joneses."

Why do people behave like this? Jealousy along with insecurity. This comparison mentality will rob you of your happiness. Nothing in life is guaranteed, but this mindset and behavior is a guarantee that you will not accumulate wealth. Imagine how it feels to be constantly comparing yourself to others and trying to one-up them. It must be both exhausting and miserable. Here is the best part. In reality, the Joneses have a zero net worth.

Do you know why the Joneses are poor but appear rich? That would be thanks to their good friend, debt, which is a powerful drug. It's like steroids. Inject yourself with steroids and go lift some weights. Wow, look how strong you are. Steroids, just like debt, are not good for you. And debt, just like steroids, will give you a one-time benefit for long-term detriment. This is a short-term boost in perception for a long–term negative reality.

When taking steroids, you probably feel great...with unlimited energy to be the envy at the gym. All your friends will see you looking really strong in pictures. The problem is that on the inside, you feel terrible because steroids will make you depressed behind closed doors. In the long term, you will fail as health problems present themselves. In the marathon of life, you just did a quick sprint to look good off the start, but will fall to the back of the pack in the race of life ahead.

This is how the Joneses are financially: they want to sprint ahead to impress those around them. When you start using debt, you will feel amazing...at first. Wow, just look at all I have; I'm so successful. You will be the envy of the block and your friend group when you pull up in your BMW. Because it's rude to ask if you actually own it, no one will ever know it's leased. But inside the Joneses household, things will start to fall apart. To keep up their image, they need new cars all the time, and they simply must have that big house and that nice furniture, whether they can afford it all or not. They will start to feel trapped because, just like being on steroids, their future is now limited because they were sprinting to borrow resources from their future.

Why waste your precious time and money trying to keep up with people like that? The answer is: you should not. For many reasons. Value is different for everyone, so you must remain focused on what *you* want. The Joneses may see value in different things than you. Clearly, they find value in renting a BMW, but you would rather own an asset. Pay no mind to those with different value sets. Jealousy fuels envy, which is the enemy of wealth.

Social media takes keeping up with the Joneses to a whole new level. Social media is such a fake environment: post only content that makes your life look perfect and amazing. Social media is a place where people post their highlight reels. Your feed is just a bunch of amazing photos, which is a breeding ground for jealousy. There are no fact checkers, or better said, "balance sheet checkers" on social media. People are free to make things look better than they really are by spending money they don't have or posting a photo from their vacation a year ago.

Understand that when you start doing things only to keep up with other people, you are losing your own identity. You lose sight of what makes you happy, which will have a ripple effect through everything in your life, including your finances. Take a step back and focus on what makes you happy, like what actually makes *you* happy. Many people attempt to create this incredible online perception when they are unhappy because it helps them mask how they feel. Again, perception is not reality.

Instead of pursuing social media acceptance, just do what makes you authentically happy. If you find the urge to compete with others online, then you might need a break from social media. Understand that the attention span of someone scrolling social media all day is a few seconds. They will look at something for a moment, and move on. Spending your energy in the hopes of impressing people on social media is not spending your time, money, or life wisely. Always remember, people only talk about wins and favorite moments in their lives; they rarely talk about the challenges.

Would you rather look like you have $1 million or actually have $1 million? I'm personally not a huge fan of looking flashy. Whether someone thinks I'm the richest person in the world or completely broke has no impact on my life. Why? Because you will never know what they truly think about you anyway. Free yourself from worrying about what others think.

Your Balance Sheet Is What Really Matters

The balance sheet is what really counts, and you will never see anyone else's balance sheet. Because you will never actually be able to compare your financial situation to anyone else's, focus on yourself. Just because someone is spending a lot of money does not mean they are rich. Don't be fooled. We know how a balance sheet works. They might not be paying cash...

The balance sheet is the ultimate financial curtain. If someone is really out of shape you can tell. They will usually be very large, cannot walk very far, etc.

A balance sheet is different. A person can be financially out of shape, but still appear to be the richest person on the block. This is of course short-term. The tide will turn on these imposters in the form of a financial recession they cannot survive, or later in retirement

When the economy is cranking and the debt is flowing like a mountain river in spring, you will see many people spending money like it's going out of style. It may puzzle you as to how they are doing this, but don't jump into the water with them.

"Be fearful when others are greedy, and be greedy when others are fearful."

—Warren Buffett

When the tide runs out, and it always does, these people suddenly go silent. The tide going out is an economic recession. Since the stock market opened, there has been an economic recession, on average, every eight years. The last recession was in 2008. As we sit today, we are enjoying *the* longest period of economic expansion ever. When the tide goes out, then, and only then, will you see who had their pants down.

This is the time to save. Don't get caught with your pants down.

During a financial recession, a negative net worth will sting you very quickly. The money is not flowing during a recession like it does in a bull market. At this point, the person creating that image through debt will no longer be able to afford the monthly payments, and that picture-perfect life will start to crumble.

A financial recession will hurt, but nothing close to entering retirement in a bad financial situation with poor financial habits. The Joneses have spent their entire life paying interest to banks on all their depreciating assets just to look cool at the start of the race. Later in life they will have little saved when they need it the most. On the flip side, the financially fit person, who was investing their money and earning compound interest, is in great shape. This is what I like to call a wealth transfer. One person is paying interest, and another is collecting it on the other side.

Focus all your energy into growing your net worth. Spend your time developing long-lasting hobbies and building long-lasting relationships with like-minded people who are encouraging about your lifestyle. Be around people you can share accomplishments with, because you are always the first to congratulate someone else. People who positively react to other people's accomplishments are generally more accomplished in their own lives. If you have Joneses in your life, rambling on about all the things they buy, ask them about their net worth. Okay, maybe don't do that, but tell them to read this book. Stay focused on what matters to you.

Stay on Budget and Be True to Yourself

I make it a game to stay on my budget. If I have change lying around and want to buy a soft drink at the gas station, I have no problem walking in with pennies to pay for it. I often get strange and annoyed looks from the cashier. Maybe they feel bad for me; maybe they think I'm poor; or maybe they are upset they have to count pennies, but who cares how you pay for something? I like to pay for things with random change I have laying around because it will not show up as spending when I update my weekly budget.

I hate to break it to you, but people really don't care what you do. If you are out to dinner, and the person you are with orders a $10 drink and yours costs $2, do you think that person will ever remember what you ordered? No. Who cares? Money is hard to make and even harder to keep. Spend it on what you value.

It's ironic, but the people seeking to impress others never really fit in. They never achieve that relationship or interaction they were looking for. Individuals who do what they want, speak their minds, and never bend or act differently based on the perceptions of others, are better liked. You need to understand that people pick up on these things and think you are coming off as inauthentic when you are trying to impress them. Be yourself, and act like the person you want to be. Don't ever be pressured by the environment you are in. You are the person with your best interests in mind, no one else.

CHAPTER 18

Financially Fit Travel

My wife and I love to travel and we take about five trips a year. This is not five trips to Bora Bora, but on average we take one large trip, about two weeks long, and four smaller trips. We've also had the same travel budget for the last four years. Since setting the original budget, our income has increased. Why not double the travel budget? Because we don't need to. We have always done everything we want on our trips, and had the time of our lives. Why would we change something that is working so well? Our trips have become a bit more extravagant, but the amount we spend on them has not changed. How is that possible? We get creative. To explain, let's start with my thoughts on credit card points and rewards programs, which is one thing we maximize for traveling.

Using Credit Card Offers

Credit cards can be the best thing in the world and the worst thing in the world. Other personal finance experts may tell you to cut them up and never use them. I'm *not* telling you to acquire a bunch of credit card debt, but if you use them in the right way, credit cards can save you boatloads of money. If you use them in the wrong way, they will cost you boatloads of money. I want to let you in on the secrets that we use.

Disclaimer: If you are just starting your road to financial fitness and consider yourself "out of shape" when it comes to finances, tread carefully. If you don't have enough cash in your bank to make a purchase, *do not*, and I will say this again, *do not put it on your credit card* because you'll just incur unnecessary interest expense. Don't think: "*I have a bonus coming next month, so I can pay it off then*." My answer is still *no*. If you don't have the cash today to cover an expense now, don't use a credit card to buy it.

When to Use a Card and When to Pay Cash

With that said, let's explore the benefits of credit cards. For starters, a great website for information on credit card offers and reward programs is the Points Guy. He has created a huge business that dives into getting the most value out of all the reward programs that different credit card companies offer. Why not take advantage of all those rewards when you are spending the money anyway? You will always need to buy food, clothes, car insurance, etc., so why not use a credit card to buy all of those things and earn cash or travel points? I buy everything I can on a credit card, as long as I'm not charged a fee for using one. If a company ever charges a fee to use a credit card, I will always pay in cash. Or if I get a discount for paying in cash, I will.

You know those big-bonus offers that credit cards always tout? You should absolutely take advantage of them if possible. We are relentless about finding the best credit card introductory offers out there, and we have paid next to nothing for flights over the years.

There are times when using a credit card is not smart. For example, my wife was getting her master's degree, and her tuition costs $4,000 each semester. I would like to pay the tuition on my credit card instead of cash because I would get 1% to 2% in a cash reward. Or I might have an introductory bonus offer if I spend $3,000 in the first three months, *but* if I use a credit card, the school will charge me a 3% processing fee. It's easy to see that it makes no sense to use a credit card in this situation.

One the flip side, I was purchasing a car from a dealer a couple years ago, and they allowed me to put $2,500 on a credit card with no transaction fee.

Rather than writing a check that day, I put $2,500 on my credit card, wrote a check for the remainder of the purchase, and paid off my credit card that next day.

Why do I recommend putting as much money on a credit card as possible? Each year my wife and I look at the credit cards with huge introductory bonus offers. Usually, you have to spend a certain amount on the card over a two- to five-month period. The introductory period rewards can range from $300 to $1,500 per card. We identify the card with the best introductory bonus offer, figure out how much we'll need to spend to receive the offer, and determine the amount of time we have in which to spend that amount. Next, we look at our budget to see when we expect to have large purchases coming up.

Once we identify the timing of any upcoming large purchases, we open the card at that time. You will also be surprised at how quickly everyday expenses like groceries and gasoline will add up. We become hyper focused and put all our expenses on the card we just opened. We were going to spend the money anyway, so we might as well get an extra $300 to $1,500 for doing so.

Side note: Don't just open a card to buy a bunch of random stuff to get the rewards. You will end up spending $1,000 to $4,000 to save $300 to $1,500. I'm no mathematician, but those numbers don't add up and just defeats the whole purpose of doing this. You have to time the introductory offer perfectly with when you budgeted for abnormally high expenditures.

How many credit cards should you have open at a specific time? Our strategy is only to have two cards open. One of the two cards is the one we have the most credit history on, we never close this card. We keep this card open for two reasons. First, the longer you have a credit line open, the better it is for your credit score. Second, credit utilization. Keeping a near zero balance on a credit line also helps your credit score. The second credit card we have is one we opened for an introductory bonus. Opening a credit card will have a minimal negative impact on your credit score. Since you are only opening this card for the introductory bonus, you will want to plan on closing it before you are charged an annual fee next year. Since you won't have a long credit history on the second card, closing it should not have a material impact to your credit score. The two card strategy will help you take advantage of great offers, all while keeping your credit score high. Everyone's financial situation is different, and your credit score will be impacted based on your specific financial situation.

VIP Airport Lounge Access

Apart from getting free flights and hotel stays, you can also get cards that grant free access to VIP lounges at airports around the world. Not only is this awesome and the only way to travel, it also saves you a bunch of money. Sometimes they have top-of-the line free booze and freshly cooked gourmet meals. Other times they just provide free coffee, nice seating, and free Wi-Fi. I always tell people that when I travel I love to hit the airport lounges; for some reason, this sounds like such a hoity-toity thing... which it is if you want to pay for it. Instead of paying for it, be creative in how you approach it. Lounges can be hit or miss, but whether you hit a good lounge or a bad lounge, it still beats sitting in uncomfortable crowded seating areas near your gate.

The best perk of the airport lounge is how much money you will save on food. Airport food sucks, and it's so overpriced. Overpriced = no value. I dislike getting food at the airport because there is absolutely no value in the pricing. When my wife and I travel, we get our meals for free at the lounges we enter for free thanks to our credit cards. We even take it a step further. We will also pack a meal to go at the lounge to have food on the plane. This extra food always holds us over until we reach our final destination. We try hit the lounge before our flight and when we land, if possible. Doing so saves us anywhere from $30 to $100 on each leg of our trip. I love doing this because the airport food is not what I'll remember about our trips. I'll remember that cool place we stumbled on and had an amazing dinner in a quaint town. We are focused on not spending a dime as we walk through the airports; we only spend money on things that we value or enrich our lives.

My best advice: hit the airport lounge when you travel: free food, coffee, water, and booze...heck yeah, I'm in for that. That way, once you get out of the spending minefield that is an airport, you can spend the money you just saved on what you love.

Budgeting for Travel

Before you even think about going anywhere, you need to make a budget. You are probably not shocked to hear me say that, but this step is so important. Most people can only take one or maybe two trips a year, so it's very important to maximize everything: your money, the location, and the memories. Head over to thirtysomethingmillionaire.com for your free Travel Budget Template, then create a top-ten list of places you want to see in the world, and start planning your next trip.

People don't often think of traveling as an investment, but it is. The person who is spending money on memories tends to be much happier than the person who spends money on material things. Material things only provide happiness for a short period of time. Travel and experiences are proven to make you happier for a longer period of time. How do you maximize your trip and your money? Unlike your household budget, we are going to start with wants and work our way down to needs. I know this sounds strange, but let's dive into the different categories you will need to contemplate.

First, come up with your total trip budget. How much did you budget for travel? Have you saved extra in other categories during the year to allocate extra money to your trip? Come up with a total dollar amount.

Next, break this budget down into sections. Build your travel budget in the same way you build your household budget. The only difference is that your travel budget will be a daily budget, and we are going to start with wants first. This is vacation, we want to spend money on the wants and get creative on the needs.

Bucket-list items: Are you going to a specific place for a specific reason? Most trips have at least one bucket-list item. Bucket-list items are the handful of must-do things on your trip, such as having dinner on the Eiffel Tower or driving a Ferrari in Italy, etc. These are often the highlights of the trip and fetch the most memories per dollar (memories = value), so we want to start here. Document those items, figure out the cost, and make "Bucket-list" the first line item in your budget.

Transportation: Let's get your flights. Find the cheapest way to get to your destination. I like to get my flights for free so I can spend more on bucket-list items or my daily SLUSH fund. I use all of the credit card offers around to ensure the total budget for my trip is not affected by this cost. Like we talked about earlier, I typically open one new card every year (keeping my oldest credit card open), and get introductory offers that cover my travel for the year. Hopefully, you will come in under budget on your flights or just get them for free.

Hotels/lodging: Get them for free with hotel points or stay in an Airbnb. We have found that Airbnb's generally offer more value than a hotel. Also, you can often stay in the middle of the city, which saves you money. How? When you stay at a hotel, everything around you is more expensive. Hotels are often surrounded by other hotels, and anything within walking distance is more expensive because it's flooded with tourists. Not only will you save money on random things you need while traveling, like food and water, but Airbnb's are typically cheaper, bigger, in better locations, and offer a more authentic experience. Hotels also often have hidden fees when you check out, such as resort charges, parking, etc... no, thank you. Don't let hidden fees reduce your bucket-list items or SLUSH fund.

You may start having to make decisions about what is important to you on your trip. If the bucket-list items, flights, and hotel took too much money out of your total, it's time to reevaluate and get creative. My wife and I never let the cost of flights or lodging hold us back. Get creative on where you sleep. You can camp, rent out a room in someone's house, couch surf, stay in a hostel, etc. Let those bucket-list items fuel your creativity and make your trip happen.

Other needs: We've knocked out the two largest expenditures. Think about what else will require an expenditure over $100 and budget for it. This is also a great place to stash a couple hundred bucks, just in case. Give your Travel Budget some flexibility.

Food: Make a daily food budget, which includes breakfast, lunch, and dinner. As a quick example, when my wife and I travel, we love getting coffee in the morning, talking about yesterday's activities, and discussing the activities ahead of us that day. We will usually find a spot where we can get a good cheap breakfast and do the same for lunch. We pack snacks purchased at a grocery store to eat throughout the day. Then at night, we can live it up and hit some really great spots for dinner. We could spend less on dinner, but that is something we love to do, so we cheap out on breakfast and lunch. Everyone is different, and if you ask yourself enough questions, or think enough about other trips you have taken, you can also sharpen your focus, which will help you identify what is important to you.

The Daily SLUSH Fund: The final line of the budget waterfall is your play money. Hopefully, you still have some dollars left over to flow into this area. Take your total travel budget and subtract the other costs we just outlined. Take that ending dollar amount and divide it by the number of days you are traveling. That is your Daily SLUSH Fund for whatever you want. Spend it all: vacation time is precious because the rest of the time you are at work. Don't be wasteful, but don't be cheap; that is why you have a budget. Track your spending daily and stay on course. If it's helpful, carry your Daily SLUSH Fund in cash each day, so when you run out, that's it. Make sure you stick to your allocated daily amount. Focus on value every second of the day to maximize those dollars.

Track your budget each day, or you will have no clue how you are tracking against the budget you set. The little things add up in real life, and when you are on vacation, they will add up even more. Think about it: when you are on vacation, all you do is walk around constantly seeing things to buy. During your real life you are stuck at work for most of the day so you are not spending money on activities.

Stick to the Budget

The more you plan for what you want to spend, the better. Stick to the plan every day, and continually ask yourself if you'll remember any potential purchases. My senses are heightened when traveling because that is when the stakes are the highest. Remain laser-focused on only spending money on things that bring the most value to your life, so you will be getting a massive return on investment (ROI) from memories to relive for years to come.

I love traveling so much that I try to save in all categories of my annual budget to make sure that I can have the trip of a lifetime every year. During the last twelve months we've traveled to Japan, Spain, France, Las Vegas, Mexico, Arizona, Chicago, Lake Tahoe, and that doesn't take into account all the small weekend trips we took. Now, think back to when I said that I have not changed my budget since the day I got out of college. The cost for me to do all of this would blow your mind, in a good way.

Believe me, you can do this as long as you plan and stay hyper focused on spending only when you see huge value. When I'm traveling, I go into hyper focus value spending mode. I will not pull out my wallet unless I know I will remember what I'm doing at this time next year. Some call it cheap, I call it resourceful, and I travel more than most people I know, and spend much less doing it every year. I have people ask me all the time, as they sip their Starbucks latte, how we afford to travel so frequently. One way I do it is by not buying Starbucks every day. I end most of my trips having a couple bucks left over in the budget. I spend it on a final pastry from our favorite café, or one last glass of wine at our favorite watering hole. That final pastry or glass of wine is ingested slowly, while enjoying the view of wherever I am in the world, feeling refreshed and full of memories that will last a lifetime.

CHAPTER 19

Relationships and Money

One of the top reasons committed relationships end in disaster is due to finances. If you have tied the knot, are thinking about it, or have a long-term partner, here is some advice to help you avoid the most common mistakes surrounding relationships and money. I will show you how having a life partner multiplies money and freedom—as long as you go about it the right way.

The person you decide to spend the rest of your life with is the single most important decision you will ever make. If you are having trouble with your partner as it relates to money, know that nothing is permanent. People can and will change, they just need the correct motivation, plan, and habits.

Money in Relationships

Remember that groupthink, according to Merriam Webster, is a pattern of thought characterized by self-deception, forced manufacture of consent, and conformity to group values and ethics. This can be both helpful and harmful.

Groupthink Situations

Any decision that is approved in a groupthink environment can be seen as a positive one by the group members, even when it's not. It's actually terrifying to see what happens to some couples who start dating. These two people are doing everything together, and soon it's okay to get out of shape, or it's okay to rack up money on credit cards. In fact, anything is okay as long as the two people agree. It doesn't have to be a verbal agreement. People are the sum of whomever they spend the most time with; you will slowly start to take on the habits of those you are around the most. If one of the two starts browsing their phone every night, the other one starts. If one of the two purchased something, then the other probably will as well. It's a vicious cycle.

Groupthink can also be positive however. Compound your money and happiness by leading through example. As long as one of the two is striving to make themselves better, the other will follow suit. Keep striving for 1% improvements. Those improvements will influence the other person, and you both will start to grow together. Small improvements compound into long-term results.

Find Activities You Love to Do Together

I advise you to make all your decisions together, large or small, to learn how to work as a team in everything you do. A great place to start is a budget. This not only teaches you how to work together, but since it's your spending road map, you will start to understand what the other person values. The first time you sit down and build a budget together, it may cause tension, but, believe me, working through this together will align your financial and spending goals and focus your money into seeking value and enjoyment. What's better than the ability to do everything you love in life with the person you love? *I cannot begin to tell you how important it is to create your annual budget with your life partner.* If you don't, your plan will most likely fail. You will get into arguments about every line in your budget. If you both sign off, then it's *our* budget.

My wife grew up differently than I did: my parents had two boys, and her parents had two girls. Our childhoods were spent doing completely different activities and hobbies. When we started dating, I made it a point to do everything together. Much of this was new for her. I knew if we didn't share a common bond, we would end up growing apart. Flash-forward a few years, and we love to travel, golf, road bike, and ski together. This has created a really strong bond and helps us maximize our money because we are funneling it into the things we *both* love. We've created economies of scale, and our dollars go further due to our common interests.

Budget for Flexible Spending

The key to success in the financially fit budget we laid out is the SLUSH Fund, along with *her* and *his* Quarterly Rations. These are the flexible dollars that you can each spend on whatever you want. As I discussed earlier in the budget section, my wife likes to spend her Quarterly Ration on getting her hair and nails done and going shopping. Last year I used the annual total of my Quarterly Ration to go snowboarding in Japan with my cousin.

As long as you spend to your budget, you can spend your money on whatever you want. This is the special sauce to budgeting because no matter what, the person you choose to spend your life with will most certainly see value in different things, and that's okay. It's expected. I have never met two people in life who enjoy or see value in exactly the same things all the time. Build your budget with your significant other to focus on expenses you can control, and plan for things that you both value. The fallout of value perception between you two is accomplished through your SLUSH fund money. Think about how many arguments can be avoided if you each had lump sum dollar amounts? As long as you stick to the total, it doesn't matter what you buy.

Our Money...Never "His" or "Her" Money

It's important to adopt an "our" money mindset when it comes to relationships. You must start thinking: *It's our money*, not his or her money. I still hear the following from couples all the time, "She can spend whatever she makes however she wants, and I get to spend what I make on whatever I want."

This is absolutely the worst way to think about money in a relationship. If you are living under the same roof or are married, you are a team; if you get a divorce, did you know the assets and debt will be split anyway? It's not his money, it's not her money, it's *our* money. What if one person is the breadwinner in the family? So what? You are still a team, act like one. Any argument you bring up, I will continue to tell you that you need to act like a team.

Communicate

Communication is by far the most important part of being a financially fit couple. You are in this boat together, you need to be 100% transparent, supportive, and collaborative. Once you have created your budget, then all that remains is walking down that spending trail map. I know that sounds easier said than done, but keep on it and keep communicating. Never hide a win or a struggle from your partner. Passed on something that was a waste of money? *Talk* about it. Overspent on something? *Talk* about it. Are you struggling staying on a budget line item? *Talk* about it. Keep the communication lines open, talk about everything, and lift each other up; become financially fit together.

Our Journey to Financial Fitness

You might be asking how you could teach a partner to live a financially fit life. I want to share a story about my wife's journey to financial fitness and what works for us.

You want to know the best thing that ever happened to us? In her first job out of college, after working sixty hours a week for ten months, my wife lost her job. This was not her fault. The company was not making enough money and was forced to lay off every analyst it had. It was a Friday, and a manager at the company pulled all the analysts into a room and told them they no longer had jobs. Tough luck. She came home in tears, and I felt very bad for her. I'm all about tough love though, and I told her, "You need to file for unemployment and start your job search."

Since *we* lost a good chunk of *our* income, we had to reduce *our* budget. Not just her spending, but both of our spending. It wasn't her income we lost, it was our income we lost. I modified our budget, and we lived sparingly until she found her next job. I loved it because it was a challenge, but it was not an easy transition for her. I got a lot of calls from her as she worked through this tough transition. Communication was so important for us, and I wanted her to know that she was not alone. I, too, had to change my lifestyle, and I didn't want her to feel like she was alone during this tough period. We could have spent more money, but that is not how you motivate yourself in a situation like this. Limiting your resources will make you hungry.

My wife had really enjoyed going to Starbucks and eating lunch out every day, and when we went out with friends she ordered expensive drinks. After losing her job, she learned that only having a Starbucks once a week meant she enjoyed it more. She cut out expensive drinks at the bar because she didn't see value in the price, and would rather not limit the number of times she went out. She also had more time on her hands, so she learned how to cook, which cut down on our grocery bill. After the initial period of struggling to learn where she found value, she became very tactical. She would save $20 at the grocery store and save some of her SLUSH fund for a new outfit. That's financial fitness at its best: spend on what you value. A new outfit is not for everyone, but saving in some areas to spend on others is financial fitness. Being let go from her first job was probably the best thing that happened to us early in our relationship. At an early stage, we forced ourselves to live on a restricted budget, which really helped us determine what we value and cut everything else out. Once she landed another job, we still had the same habits, and that has carried us to where we are today. We focus on what brings value to our lives, figure out how to accomplish it all in our budget, and then save the rest.

This positive change in money behavior goes both ways. Before I met my wife, I had an unhealthy relationship with money; I went to extremes *not* to spend it, which is also not healthy. Meeting her has balanced me to better understand what is worth spending money on and what isn't. This, I know, is a strange issue to have with money.

To end my marriage counseling session, I want to say it's important to make sure you think about the other person before yourself. I know it sounds cliché, and you were probably not expecting this from a personal finance book, but hang in there with me. When it comes to my SLUSH fund money and my Quarterly Ration, I would rather give it to my wife. If you asked my wife about her Quarterly Ration budget or her SLUSH fund budget, she would rather give it to me. We always think about each other first. Guess what happens when behavior like this is combined? Each person gets what they truly want because the other person is looking out for them, rather than the self-centered version of only looking out for yourself.

How to Help Each Other Win and Become Financially Aligned

We are both financially fit people now. I have always been like this, but it took my wife a few years to adopt this way of thinking about money. How did she become the financially fit person she is today? We created and updated our weekly budget together. I worked with her to help her narrow her focus to what she *actually* wanted rather than what she *thought* she wanted. I would then lay out a forecast of our money over the next year to show her the impact that our positive money mindset today would have on our future. It's important to help explain the *why* for your partner to understand the concept better.

My wife and I try to sit down for at least thirty minutes each day, usually over dinner, to chat about money, life, investing, passions, work, or anything else that is on our minds. Apart from solidifying our marriage, it really helps us understand what is important to *us* and what we would like to accomplish. I urge you to find time every day to have those types of conversations, which will lead you to dial in what is important and keep you motivated to work toward your goals.

The best part about our daily conversations? It helps us create and fine-tune future plans for investing and shared experiences. If we want to do something within the next five years, we make it a monthly priority to set aside money for when the time is right, so we can pounce. Our plans can change, but with enough conversations, we can shed light on the right course of action. Planning is also very therapeutic; it keeps you energized and engaged. Life is all about having something to work toward, and something to look forward to, as well as reflecting on wonderful past memories. Paint the picture of the life you want in the future to motivate you and your partner to have financially fit money habits today.

Set Rewards

Seriously, why do all of this if you don't get a reward? Most budget books will tell you that being debt free is enough of a reward. I say you need to treat yourself at certain milestones. In our household, we reward ourselves quarterly. If we hit our net-worth goal, we each get something. Since traveling is important to us, we usually combine our "somethings" and plan a trip. The reward you choose can be anything. Think about it every day and use that to fuel your ambition and hit your goals. You are a team, and together you can double your efforts for double the effect.

Dual Income

This might be a sore subject for some people, but in the world we live in today, having a dual-household income is often a necessity. I know many families who have kids and one person stays at home. That's perfectly fine, but you need to understand how much that can cost you over the long-term before you commit to that decision. This is another conversation about understanding the total cost; it's more than you might think.

Did you know the USDA estimates having a child today will cost you, on average, more than $230,000 from birth to age seventeen?[18] This may seem like a large number. Yes, but let me blow your mind a little bit more. $230,000 is the tip of the iceberg of the actual cost. That $230,000 figure doesn't even include college; mind blowing, I know. You know what else this doesn't include? A parent taking time off work.

People think that the only cost of taking a couple years off work to raise kids is the loss of income during those years, and that you save a lot of money by not having to pay for daycare. What they are not taking into account is the long-term impact of missing those peak-earning years. If you make $50,000 a year, and you decide to take three years off work. Math class: what does this cost you? If you said $150,000, you are wrong. You're not taking into account the fact that you are removing yourself from the workforce during one of the most high-growth advancement stages of your career.

At some point in your career, your percentage increase in salary will start to level out. Think about it. You get out of college and think you are making a lot of money. If you work hard, you can double that in a couple of years. Later in life the percentage increases will level out. You will not continue to see 100% increases in your salary over a short period of time. When you just get into the workplace, you are in the learning and developing stage and are not

---

[18] USDA, "The Cost of Raising a Child," updated March 6, 2017, https://www.usatoday.com/story/money/personalfinance/2018/02/26/raising-child-costs-233-610-you-financially-prepared-parent/357243002/.

very valuable to a company. Over the next ten years, you will start to refine your skills and with refined skills comes more money.

Back to our example of earning $50,000 and taking three years off to raise children. How much will it really cost you? Drum roll please... it could cost you anywhere from seven to ten times your current salary. Wow that is a big number. Let's break that down a little. Raising a child is not easy and is very demanding, but unfortunately it's not something you can put on your résumé when you rejoin the workforce. With that in mind, you need to know that when you enter the job market again, you will most likely take a step down in salary from what you were earning a couple years prior. This affects you every year for the rest of your life. Let's say you take a salary that is 15% to 25% lower than what you were earning three years ago, you will be making 15% to 25% lower next year and the year after that. In fact, you may have that income difference for most of your career. As you now know, money compounds over your entire life. The impact of this income gap by the time you turn sixty is significant.

Additionally, during that time you took off work, you also weren't contributing to a retirement account, and your partner most likely had to reduce the amount they contributed to their retirement accounts. Think back to compound interest. If you stopped working at age twenty-five, each dollar you would have contributed beginning at age twenty-five would have increased by 14.8 times. Contributing less during those years will absolutely have a massive impact at retirement. Giving up those key years of investing is huge. I know this seems crazy, but it gets even more painful. Remember how those years are the highest growth years of your career? One of the biggest growth factors in your career are the relationships you build. Once you build solid relationships at a company, it becomes the point at which your career will take off because you have gained the trust to work on higher-level projects, which in turn leads to higher-level paychecks. Missing out on those years can have a huge impact on your life later; these are the years when you can set the base for your career to explode.

I'm not advocating for or against having kids or staying home to raise children versus working. I only want you to know the total cost. I understand daycare is expensive, but that pales in comparison to giving up seven to ten times of your current salary. Daycare is cheap when compared to taking time off work while you are young.

It goes without saying, but there are many things you can do to be ready for adding children to your family. My wife and I don't currently have kids, but we have a plan in place for when we do. Your real objective here is to set up your finances in a way that doesn't have to change if/when you do have children.

I know it's really exciting when you start to make money. You suddenly have the ability to buy cars and houses or take lavish vacations. Before you do anything, answer these questions:

1. If I lost my job, would I need to cut back in any area?
2. If I had kids, would I need to cut back in any area?

Your answer should be *no* to both. We know children are expensive, so make sure you kick up your safety net savings fund to at least nine months of savings, buy a home with a mortgage that is less than 30% of your take-home pay (take-home pay includes 15% savings like we discussed earlier), and pay off your debt (mortgage excluded here)—then it will be an easier transition into parenthood.

CHAPTER 20

Final Thoughts

I want to thank you for reading this book. Treat it as your road map not only to financial freedom, but also a map to help you find the things in life you love. This will allow you to focus on building the correct habits that will lead to a lifetime of happiness and wealth. I will leave you with the following two things to think about.

Credit Score Freedom

Get to the point where your credit score doesn't matter. I will never forget the day I was talking with the CFO of my company, who was mad about being overcharged for a particular service. He first tried to negotiate the bill to what was fair, but he couldn't come to an agreement with the vendor. The bill was then sent to a collections agency, which, in turn, hurt his credit score. It was early in my career, and I was looking to buy a house, so I asked him if he was worried about his credit score.

He answered, "I don't care about my credit score because I will never use credit again." He had two homes, each worth over a million dollars that were paid for in cash. He had a large investment account and a healthy cash savings account. He worked because he enjoyed the grind and challenge of a high-profile job, not because he needed the money. His comment about not

189

needing credit really sunk in for me. A high credit score is something a lot of people brag about, but all a good credit score means is that you are good at having debt. That is it.

I'm not saying that you should go out and tank your credit score. Rather, I'm saying that, at some point, you should not need to borrow money. That is the goal: be your own bank. That is financial freedom. Credit should be a tool used while you are young as you establish a solid financial base. Student loans get you the high-paying job, but after you pay off your loans, you will never need them again. Your first home, first car etc. When you are young, you are typically not making a lot of money, and through the next couple years, you will have the highest percentage growth in your income. As you get settled and grow your income, you should be able to pay off any debt. After you pay it off once, you should never need it again. Don't use debt to overconsume; use debt to help build your foundation.

Keep your credit score as high as possible while building your financial foundation, then become the person who can say you don't care about your credit score because you are the bank! This was an extreme example, and even if you are your own bank, it's a good practice to pay for what you consume. A good credit score is a great tool when you are in a pinch, or want to take advantage of a great real estate investment opportunity. Or, you can be the guy worth millions and tell them to go pound sand.

Being Weird Is Cool

Plan for and only spend money on things you see value in and never ever, ever care about what people think about you. Be the odd duck that is very stubborn. Once you start accumulating wealth, the people who may have said negative things to you in the past will suddenly change their tune. Stay humble, but never hide the accomplishments you worked so hard for. Once you are financially fit, the most important thing you can do is teach and help others to do the same thing. Spread the word, and teach the habits that helped you build wealth while living the life of your dreams. Have your biggest problem be deciding how to spend your money. Let the only anxiety in your life be which third car you want to buy. Let any negativity just sail right on past you. Down this road, you will face a lot of different feedback from people around you.

When on the road to financial fitness, some people will cheer you on; some may think you're broke for not spending money; some will be jealous of you; and some people will look up to you, but regardless, you will be respected.

People love being around those who can make a confident decision. Be the odd duck: look for money under the mattress at a hotel room, pick up that penny in front of people who you just met, smuggle booze into movie theaters and concerts, and use all the money you save to spend only where you see value. Live the life you've always dreamed of. Money is a precious commodity; treat it like one, and only spend toward things that enrich your life. Save the rest. I truly love my life, and my goal is to share my experiences so you can become a millionaire and enjoy your life both now and in the future.

To keep up with us, please go to thirtysomethingmillionaire.com, and check us out on Instagram and Facebook @thirtysomethingmillionaire.

Signing off,
The Thirty Something Millionaire

ABOUT THE AUTHOR

As a competitive snowboarder at a young age, Cory still loves the adrenaline of extreme sports. Cory is a Colorado native and enjoys spending time outdoors in his home state as well as traveling the world. He is a car enthusiast with a passion for working on cars and following Formula 1 racing.

With extensive experience consulting clients one on one, Cory has created plans that set his clients up for success with their personal finances. Thirty Something Millionaire was created to expand the reach of Cory's personal finance principles. His primary focus is basic financial structure with an emphasis on life and wealth maximization.

Cory received a bachelor's degree in Business Administration with a concentration in finance from Colorado State University. Over the past 10 years, he has worked as a corporate finance professional in various roles for billion-dollar organizations. Cory has also consulted for start-up businesses assisting in financial reporting, analysis, and strategic long-term planning.

Cory lives in Denver, Colorado, with his wife Treslyn Roberts, and their two dogs.

Made in the USA
Monee, IL
07 January 2020